Blueprints for Modern Success

Timeless Strategies for Thriving in a Modern World

Emma Lawson

Table of Contents

The Timeless Pursuit of Success	1
The Power of Desire	6
The Foundation of Success	7
Case Study: Sara Blakely's Journey	10
Crafting Your Desire Statement	14
Final Insights	18
Faith in Your Vision	20
Understanding Faith in Vision	21
Case Study: Elon Musk's Visionary Pursuits	24
Strategies for Cultivating Faith	28
Final Insights	32
Specialized Knowledge	34
The Importance of Acquiring Specialized Knowledge	35
Case Study: Simone Biles—Mastering Gymnastics Through Relentless Learning and Practice	40
Action Steps: Identifying Knowledge Gaps and Developing a Learning Plan	44
Summary and Reflections	47
Imagination as Your Workshop	49
Ideas and Creativity: The Seeds of Wealth	50
Case Study: Reed Hastings and Netflix	54
Brainstorming: A Tool for Innovation	58
Vision Boards: Visualizing Success	62

Concluding Thoughts	65
Organized Planning	67
Vision to Action	68
Strategic Planning at Facebook	71
Breaking Down Long-Term Goals	74
Actionable Steps and Deadlines	77
Bringing It All Together	81
The Mastermind Alliance	83
The Power of Supportive Teams	84
Case Study: Steve Jobs and Steve Wozniak	88
Identifying Potential Mentors and Collaborators	91
Action Steps for Building Your Mastermind Alliance	94
Bringing It All Together	96
Persistence Through Adversity	98
Understanding the Nature of Adversity	99
Lessons from Oprah Winfrey's Journey	102
Developing Resilience Through Journaling	106
Reframing Failures as Lessons Learned	110
Final Insights	114
Overcoming Fear and Doubt	116
The Nature of Fear	117
Richard Branson's Case Study	120
Identifying Personal Fears	124
Taking Incremental Steps	127
Transforming Fear into Motivation	131
Bringing It All Together	134

- The Subconscious Mind and Success — 136
  - Programming Your Mind for Achievement — 137
  - Case Study: Kobe Bryant's Visualization Techniques — 142
  - Action Steps: Cultivating a Meditation Practice — 145
  - Creating a Mindful Environment — 149
  - Adopting a Growth Mindset — 151
  - Final Insights — 155
- Beyond Wealth: Redefining Success — 157
  - Purpose as a Core Component of Success — 158
  - The Role of Relationships in Achieving Success — 161
  - Impact as a Measure of Success — 164
  - Case Study: Melinda French Gates' Philanthropic Mission — 167
  - Taking Action: Reflecting on Legacy and Crafting a Mission Statement — 171
  - Summary and Reflections — 175
- Your Roadmap to Prosperity — 177

Chapter 1
The Timeless Pursuit of Success

In every era, humanity has been captivated by the pursuit of success—a relentless quest that transcends time and culture. From ancient philosophers to modern-day innovators, the desire to achieve greatness has remained a constant force driving individuals to break barriers and redefine possibilities. Yet, while the essence of success retains its allure, the means to achieving it have evolved dramatically. The industrial revolution heralded iconic figures like Andrew Carnegie and John D. Rockefeller, masters of industry who epitomized success in their time. Today, we look to the stories of tech entrepreneurs, influencers, and socially conscious leaders who navigate an increasingly complex world—a world marked not just by economic and technological change but also by profound social transformation.

This book embarks on an exploration of the universal principles that underpin success, while shedding light on how these age-old truths can be adapted to meet the unique challenges and opportunities of the contemporary landscape. What does it mean to be successful in an interconnected digital age? How do we balance economic ambition with a growing awareness of social responsibility? These questions encapsulate the core theme of this work: deciphering success in today's multifaceted world.

Success stories of the past often depict singular triumphs driven by visionary thinking and unwavering determination. Napoleon Hill's seminal work on personal achievement drew lessons from the era's titans of business—individuals whose legacies were built upon steel, railroads, and financial empires. Their world was characterized by tangible production and expansive growth, where success was measured primarily in material wealth and industrial expansion. But as we step into the present, the parameters of success have broadened, encompassing not only economic prosperity but also innovation, influence, and ethical leadership.

Our journey begins by recognizing the shifts that define modern success. The digital revolution has birthed a new breed of entrepreneurs who harness technology's potential to create value and drive progress. Visionaries like Steve Jobs and Elon Musk have redefined entire industries, not merely through the products they've introduced, but through the sheer audacity of their vision. Social media influencers reach millions, shaping opinions and trends across the globe with unprecedented immediacy. Meanwhile, leaders focused on societal impact and sustainability remind us of our collective responsibility to foster positive change.

Today's aspiring individuals must navigate this landscape with agility, foresight, and a willingness to embrace change. This book promises to equip readers with practical tools that resonate with the realities of our times. Through real-world examples and actionable insights, it aims to empower you to harness your potential and transform both your personal and financial aspirations into enduring success.

By delving into these stories and strategies, you'll gain a deeper understanding of how timeless principles manifest in today's dynamic environment. You'll discover that while the methods may evolve, certain fundamentals remain steadfast: the power of clarity in vision, the discipline of persistence, and the importance of adaptability in the face of unforeseen challenges. These elements form the bedrock of accomplishment, no matter the age or context.

Moreover, success is no longer a solitary pursuit—it thrives within communities and networks, fueled by collaboration and shared goals. This book underscores the significance of building connections, fostering trust, and cultivating relationships that propel you towards your objectives. Whether you're an entrepreneur launching a startup, a professional advancing your career, a student setting out on a new academic journey, or a dreamer envisioning the future, the principles discussed will guide you toward realizing your potential.

In embracing these insights, you'll learn how to create a roadmap that aligns with your unique purpose and values. The narrative doesn't just draw from those who have reached the pinnacle of success but also includes lessons learned from setbacks and failures. Every misstep contains valuable wisdom, teaching us resilience and the fortitude to rise again stronger.

In the ensuing pages, prepare to be inspired by stories that exemplify the spirit of perseverance, ingenuity, and transformation. Let them ignite the fire within you, urging you to keep pushing boundaries and redefining what success means to you. With each chapter, you'll gather tools that fuel your journey, ensuring that your efforts are sustainable and impactful.

In conclusion, this introduction is but the beginning of a conversation between you and the timeless pursuit of success. As you turn the pages, allow yourself to absorb, reflect, and apply the knowledge woven throughout. May this book serve as a compass guiding you toward your ambitions, encouraging you to leverage the rich tapestry of insights presented herein.

The path to success is an evolving narrative—one that beckons you to participate and shape its course. By engaging with the material in this book, you undertake an adventure that honors tradition while embracing innovation, and recognizes the limitless potential that lies within your grasp. Herein lies the promise to you, dear reader: together, we will embark on a transformative journey, uncovering the blueprint for lasting personal and financial success in a world full of opportunities waiting to be seized.

Chapter 2
The Power of Desire

Desire is a powerful force that ignites our capabilities and propels us toward achieving great feats. It is the initial push on our journey from where we are to where we wish to be. This emotion, deeply embedded within, is more than just a wish or fleeting thought; it becomes the driver behind the extraordinary efforts people make to fulfill personal and professional aspirations. For anyone aiming for success, desire often serves as the compass guiding their actions and decisions, defining their path in a world filled with opportunities and challenges alike.

In this chapter, readers will explore how desire sets the stage for achievement and transforms ambition into reality. The text delves into how this potent motivator acts as the foundation for goal setting, persistence, and resilience. It examines various scenarios, including entrepreneurship and sports, where desire plays a pivotal role in overcoming obstacles and maintaining focus amidst adversity. Through real-life examples and insights, the chapter illuminates how desire not only energizes individuals but also provides clarity and direction on their journey to success. By understanding and nurturing this crucial element, readers can learn to harness its power to unlock their full potential and achieve remarkable outcomes.

The Foundation of Success

Desire is a powerful force that propels individuals toward their goals. It serves as the initial spark of motivation, igniting a path that leads to achievement and success. This intrinsic drive is often what differentiates those who merely wish for change from those who actively pursue it. Desire is not just a fleeting thought or a passing fancy; it is a deep-seated emotion that fuels action. When individuals possess a strong desire, they are more likely to take the necessary steps toward achieving their aspirations.

To understand the impact of desire, consider its role as a catalyst. Imagine an entrepreneur with a vision to create a groundbreaking product. The journey from concept to reality is arduous and filled with challenges. However, it is the persistent desire to see this vision come to life that pushes the individual to keep going. This desire acts as the driving force behind every decision, every late night, and every sacrifice made along the way.

Moreover, desire shapes one's mindset, instilling the perseverance required to overcome obstacles. The road to achievement is seldom smooth, and the ability to remain resilient in the face of adversity often hinges on the strength of one's desire. A determined mindset is crucial for navigating setbacks and failures, which are inevitable components of any ambitious pursuit. For instance, athletes training for the Olympics face grueling schedules and intense competition. Their unwavering desire for victory compels them to push through pain and exhaustion, ultimately enabling them to reach peak performance levels.

Without desire, efforts may lack direction or intensity. When there is no burning passion driving an endeavor, the likelihood of achieving significant accomplishments diminishes. Desire provides clarity, focusing attention on specific goals and ensuring that energy and resources are directed purposefully. Consider someone attempting to learn a new skill, such as playing an instrument. Without a genuine desire to master it, practice sessions may become inconsistent, and progress slow, leading to discouragement and eventual abandonment of the goal.

Furthermore, desire sets the stage for effective goal setting by clarifying what one truly wishes to achieve. It serves as the foundation upon which realistic and achievable objectives are built. By clearly defining their desires, individuals can translate abstract aspirations into tangible targets. This clarity allows for the formulation of actionable plans, outlining the steps necessary to reach desired outcomes. A student aiming for top grades, for example, must first identify the desire to excel academically before creating a study schedule that aligns with their goal.

The relationship between desire and goal setting also highlights the importance of introspection and self-awareness. To leverage desire effectively, one must engage in honest reflection to uncover what truly matters to them. This process helps distinguish between superficial wants and genuine desires that resonate deeply. Once these true desires are identified, individuals can align their actions with their core values and passions, fostering a sense of fulfillment and purpose.

In addition, the strength of desire can be influenced by external factors, such as environment and social support. Being surrounded by like-minded individuals who share similar aspirations can amplify personal desire, creating a sense of accountability and encouragement. Conversely, negative influences or unsupportive environments may dampen one's enthusiasm and hinder progress. Therefore, cultivating a supportive network and seeking inspiration from others can enhance the power of desire in one's journey toward success.

When harnessed effectively, desire becomes a transformative force, enabling individuals to realize their potential and achieve remarkable feats. It drives innovation, creativity, and perseverance, pushing boundaries and challenging limits. The stories of accomplished individuals across various fields often reveal a common thread: a deep-rooted desire that propelled them to greatness.

Case Study: Sara Blakely's Journey

Sara Blakely's journey to creating Spanx is a compelling illustration of desire in action. It began with her identifying an unmet need in the market, which was rooted in her personal frustration with existing products. As she prepared for a party one evening, Sara found herself dissatisfied with how her white pants looked. The panty lines were visible and unflattering, and traditional shapewear options were either uncomfortable or ineffective. This common problem sparked a desire within her to find a solution, not just for herself but for countless others facing the same issue.

Driven by this desire, Sara embarked on a mission to innovate. Her creativity led her to cut the feet off a pair of control-top pantyhose, which gave her the smooth appearance she wanted without any visible lines. This homemade solution was the inception of Spanx, a product that would soon revolutionize the shapewear industry. But the path from concept to market was far from straightforward. Sara faced numerous rejections along the way. Many manufacturers were skeptical about her idea, dismissing it as trivial or impractical. However, her unwavering desire to bring her vision to life fueled her resilience.

She persevered, continually pitching her idea despite the setbacks. Her commitment paid off when she eventually got a manufacturer to produce her product. With this breakthrough, Sara focused on introducing Spanx to potential buyers. Persistence remained her ally as she navigated the challenges of marketing a new product. She boldly approached Neiman Marcus, demonstrating the product's effectiveness in a ladies' restroom—a move that later secured her first major retail deal.

As Spanx gained traction, it quickly became evident that Sara's desire was not merely about solving a personal frustration but also about empowering women. Her story underscores the transformative power of desire, showing how it can turn a simple idea into a billion-dollar empire through persistence and creativity. Sara's initial frustration led to a product that brought confidence to many, highlighting how personal experiences and emotions can serve as powerful catalysts for innovation.

With every step she took, from design to production to sale, her desire was the driving force that pushed her forward. Despite being new to the fashion and retail industries, Sara taught herself everything she needed to know, displaying a commitment that only a profound desire could sustain. She invested her own savings into the company, betting on her belief that Spanx could succeed. Through sheer determination, she managed to navigate unfamiliar territories, learning the intricacies of business operations and marketing strategies.

The impact of her creation extended beyond financial success. Spanx set new standards in the fashion world, prompting established brands to reconsider their offerings in response to consumer demand. Moreover, Blakely's triumph served as inspiration for aspiring entrepreneurs, particularly women who saw in her story the potential to transform obstacles into opportunities. By transforming her experience into a thriving enterprise, Sara Blakely showed that with desire, coupled with determination and ingenuity, almost anything is possible.

Her journey also emphasizes the importance of staying true to one's vision, even when faced with doubt and rejection. Sara's unwavering belief in her product, fueled by her original desire, empowered her to endure the uncertainties of entrepreneurship. Her ability to remain steadfast in the face of skepticism exemplifies how a strong desire can act as a guiding light, steering individuals towards their goals despite external challenges.

Furthermore, Sara's story reveals how desire can provoke societal change. By creating Spanx, she not only addressed a practical issue but also initiated conversations about comfort, confidence, and body positivity. This broader impact underscores how desire can extend beyond personal achievement to influence collective mindsets, proving that one person's vision can indeed have a lasting effect on the world.

Crafting Your Desire Statement

Harnessing the power of desire begins by solidifying our deepest wishes in a tangible form. One effective approach to achieving this is through the practice of writing a 'Definitive Desire Statement.' This exercise involves clearly defining what you want and encapsulating those aspirations into concise, powerful phrases. This statement becomes more than just words on paper; it is a blueprint for your future endeavors, serving as a focal point around which all your ambitions converge.

Creating a Definitive Desire Statement is akin to sculpting your dreams into reality. When you translate your desires from thoughts to written word, they become more concrete, helping you visualize your goals with clarity. Just like an artist sees their creation before painting on the canvas, your desires need that clarity before they can manifest into genuine achievements. It offers a moment of introspection: What do you genuinely wish to achieve? How does this ambition align with the person you envision becoming?

Upon articulating your desires, there's a transformative shift within. The act of writing these statements boosts motivation, fueling actions towards achieving them. Your desires no longer remain abstractions but evolve into actionable objectives. Imagine you're steering a ship at sea; your desire statement acts like navigational coordinates, steering every decision, ensuring that even when faced with challenges, your ship remains steadfast on course. Knowing precisely what you yearn for fosters determination and provides the necessary grit to pursue your dreams despite obstacles or detours.

However, desires are not static. As life progresses, experiences inform and sometimes alter our ambitions. Regularly reviewing and revising your Definitive Desire Statement ensures it reflects your evolving aspirations. Think of it as tending to a garden; regular care is essential if one wishes to reap a bountiful harvest. Similarly, assessing this statement allows you to check if your goals align with where you stand today and where you wish to head tomorrow. Periodic reflection ensures that your ambitions remain relevant and aligned with both personal growth and external changes.

A well-defined desire statement serves another critical function—it acts as a compass, directing your choices towards pathways that align with ultimate outcomes. Much like how a compass always points north, anchoring decisions in this statement guarantees they guide you closer to your desired destination. In moments of uncertainty, whether choosing between opportunities or facing setbacks, this statement will be your steadfast reference, helping prioritize efforts and resources efficiently.

Beyond providing direction, the statement also imbues your goals with purpose, which in turn shapes priorities. Consider professionals like entrepreneurs who juggle countless responsibilities daily. Their time is finite; thus, aligning tasks with their desire statement maximizes productivity and impact. For instance, if an entrepreneur's statement emphasizes innovation, then efforts should focus on fostering creativity within their team and environment. Every decision, big or small, becomes a stepping stone towards fulfilling that overarching aim.

By cultivating such alignment, individuals avoid the pitfalls of indecision or distraction, often the precursors to unmet goals. The statement simplifies complex choices, clarifying what's truly significant amidst life's noise. When confronted with enticing but unrelated opportunities, ask yourself: Does this align with my definitive desires? If not, perhaps it detracts from valuable time better spent pursuing passions genuinely resonant with your core objectives.

It is worth noting, though, that crafting an effective statement requires introspection and honesty. Engaging deeply with oneself might unearth hidden fears or doubts regarding ambitions. Yet confronting these elements is vital for authenticity, ensuring your desire statement genuinely represents personal truths rather than societal expectations or superficial influences. Remember, the strength of your statement lies in its sincerity—only then can it effectively guide and inspire.

Ultimately, this practice is not restricted to any particular group; it transcends age or profession. Whether you're a student envisioning future careers or an established professional seeking new ventures, defining your desires lays a strong foundation from which to launch growth and achievement. Such articulation empowers individuals across all walks of life to chase after goals ardently and deliberately, turning dreams into attainable realities.

Final Insights

Desire, as we've explored in this chapter, is much more than just a wish; it is the foundation upon which all achievements are built. Desire drives us from idea to action, serving as the motivation behind every step we take towards our goals. By examining examples like Sara Blakely's journey with Spanx, we see how desire can push us through obstacles and bring about world-changing innovations. Her story demonstrates that when our intentions are deeply rooted, the desire becomes an unstoppable force, guiding us even through uncertainty and rejection. This intrinsic drive shapes our mindset, enabling perseverance and resilience in the face of challenges.

As you reflect on your own ambitions, consider how desire plays a role in shaping your path. Crafting a Definitive Desire Statement can help anchor your aspirations, providing clarity and direction. Regularly revisiting this statement ensures your goals remain aligned with your evolving self, akin to adjusting a compass for a clear course. Remember, desire not only propels personal success but can also instigate broader societal change. By nurturing a strong, authentic desire, you can embark on a purposeful journey toward achieving significant milestones, transforming dreams into reality.

Chapter 3
Faith in Your Vision

Faith in one's vision serves as a cornerstone for turning dreams into reality. It is a guiding force that shapes how individuals perceive their goals and the challenges they encounter along the way. This faith operates subtly yet powerfully, steering mindset and behavior towards a path of achievement. It is about seeing potential in situations others might overlook and finding strength in moments of doubt. When deeply embedded, this belief becomes an integral part of how one navigates life's terrain, offering not just motivation but also resilience in the face of adversity.

The chapter delves into how faith transforms aspirations into tangible outcomes, exploring its role as a catalyst for success. It takes readers on a journey through real-world examples, illustrating how unwavering belief can inspire change and innovation. The text examines the nuanced ways faith influences decision-making and problem-solving, turning obstacles into opportunities. By understanding this dynamic, readers will learn to harness their faith in practical ways to achieve their personal and professional goals. The discussion includes strategies for cultivating and sustaining this belief, emphasizing clarity of purpose and the importance of a supportive environment. Through these insights, the chapter aims to equip ambitious individuals with the tools needed to keep their vision alive and thriving.

Understanding Faith in Vision

Faith in personal vision is a powerful force that can transform an individual's dreams into reality. At its core, faith shapes the outcomes of one's efforts by influencing mindset and behavior. This influence occurs subtly, guiding decision-making processes and enabling individuals to see opportunities where others may see barriers. When a person has deep-rooted belief in their goals, it alters the way they perceive challenges. Rather than viewing setbacks as insurmountable, they become stepping stones or lessons on the path to success.

The role of faith in shaping outcomes cannot be overstated. It fundamentally affects how individuals approach problems and solutions. With this belief, a person is more likely to maintain a positive attitude even when faced with difficulties. This positivity breeds resilience, which is crucial for overcoming obstacles that might seem overwhelming at first glance. When someone believes in their vision, they are more motivated to keep pushing forward, experimenting with different strategies until they find one that works. This persistence often results in achieving objectives that initially seemed out of reach.

Consider the act of consistent belief. It acts as a compass, keeping an individual aligned with their ultimate goal no matter how stormy the journey becomes. Coupled with unwavering determination, consistent belief allows people to tackle challenges from a place of calm assurance rather than anxiety or doubt. This mental state is vital because it opens up pathways toward innovation and creative problem-solving. An entrepreneur, for instance, can look at market shortages not as dead ends but as opportunities to introduce new products or services, transforming obstacles into assets.

One of the most significant advantages faith provides is its ability to enable risk-taking. In business and life alike, many great successes have been borne out of the willingness to take calculated risks. Faith is the driving force behind this readiness to explore unknown territories and challenge conventional wisdom. It empowers individuals to step outside their comfort zones, paving the way for groundbreaking innovations and unconventional solutions. This kind of boldness could lead to pioneering new industries or revolutionizing existing practices, setting the stage for monumental achievements.

Real-world examples abound of how strong belief systems have resulted in societal advancements. History is replete with figures who, driven by faith in their visions, pushed boundaries and catalyzed change. Think of leaders in civil rights movements or inventors who changed the course of technology. Their faith did not just fuel their pursuit; it inspired countless others to believe in their capacity for transformative impact. Such stories underscore the far-reaching effects of having faith in one's vision—not only changing an individual's life but also leaving a lasting mark on society.

In practice, developing and sustaining faith in one's vision involves a few essential steps. First, it requires clarity of purpose. Understanding what you want to achieve and why it matters creates a solid foundation for belief. Moreover, surrounding oneself with supportive individuals who reinforce this vision helps sustain motivation when times get tough. Finally, engaging in regular self-reflection and visualization can bolster faith, making it easier to stay committed to the path ahead.

Case Study: Elon Musk's Visionary Pursuits

Elon Musk stands as a quintessential example of someone whose faith in his vision has profoundly transformed industries and our perception of the future. Central to this transformation is Musk's unwavering belief in sustainable energy and interplanetary travel. These ideas aren't just dreams to him—rather, they are driving forces behind some of the most innovative projects of our time. At Tesla, his vision for a world less reliant on fossil fuels has pushed the boundaries of what's possible with electric vehicles and renewable energy solutions. Meanwhile, at SpaceX, Musk's ambition to make humans a multiplanetary species is reshaping how we think about space exploration and its potential to preserve and expand humanity.

Musk's journey hasn't been without its share of setbacks and skepticism from both industry experts and the general public. Many doubted the feasibility of mass-market electric cars or the practicality of launching reusable rockets. Financial struggles, technical challenges, and fierce competition threatened to derail his endeavors multiple times. However, Musk's conviction remained steadfast through these trials. His ability to maintain focus on his broader goals, despite immediate obstacles, illustrates a crucial aspect of believing in one's vision: perseverance. Rather than succumbing to doubt, Musk uses it as fuel to propel his projects forward, often exceeding expectations and silencing critics along the way.

The impact of Musk's visions extends beyond overcoming personal and professional hurdles; it's about disrupting entire industries and creating opportunities where none existed before. Tesla, once a small startup, is now a key player in the automotive industry, pushing major manufacturers to accelerate their own investment in electric vehicles. Similarly, SpaceX has not only reduced the cost of accessing space but has also inspired a renewed interest in lunar and Martian exploration among competitors and governments worldwide. By challenging existing paradigms, Musk's ventures have opened the door to new markets, prompting innovation that benefits society at large.

Outside of mere market disruption, Musk's story exemplifies how visionary faith can catalyze transformative change on a global scale. This change isn't limited to technology but extends to societal shifts in how we address environmental issues and explore the cosmos. It's a reminder that steadfast belief in a powerful vision can lead to outcomes that were once deemed impossible. His work has influenced policies, encouraged public debates about sustainability and space colonization, and inspired a generation of entrepreneurs and innovators to dream bigger and aim higher.

In essence, Musk's journey underscores the critical role that faith in one's vision plays in achieving groundbreaking success. While technical prowess and business acumen are undoubtedly essential, it is the fundamental belief in the possibility of change that acts as the catalyst for progress. Each step Musk takes, whether it's launching a rocket or rolling out a new vehicle model, is rooted in a deep-seated confidence that the future he envisions is not just possible but inevitable. This mindset serves as a powerful lesson for anyone looking to transform their dreams into reality.

In analyzing Musk's path, several themes become apparent. Firstly, his belief system is not static; it evolves as he learns and adapts to new information and technology. This adaptability allows him to refine his vision over time, aligning it more closely with emerging possibilities and contingencies.

Secondly, Musk actively seeks out challenges, viewing them as opportunities to test the limits of his beliefs and stretch the boundary of what his companies can achieve. Lastly, he surrounds himself with individuals who share his ambitious vision, building teams that are not only skilled but are also deeply invested in the company's mission. This collaborative effort amplifies the impact of his faith, as each team member contributes towards turning vision into reality.

Moreover, Musk's approach to risk highlights another facet of having faith in one's vision. He is known for his willingness to take significant risks, often investing his own money and resources into unproven technologies and uncertain markets. This readiness to walk the talk reflects a profound trust in the eventual success of his ventures. It is this level of commitment that sets visionary leaders apart from those who may falter under pressure or uncertainty. By betting on his beliefs, Musk demonstrates that true faith in a vision means being ready to embrace potential failure as a stepping stone toward ultimate success.

As Musk continues to push the envelope, his journey serves as an inspiring narrative of how visionary faith can drive substantial and meaningful change. His story is not merely about technological advancements but about the broader implications of holding and nurturing a vision with dedication and vigor. For anyone striving to achieve personal and financial success, Musk's example underscores the importance of clarity, resilience, and unwavering belief in the power of one's ideas.

Strategies for Cultivating Faith

In the journey of transforming visions into reality, maintaining faith in one's goals is both a powerful motivator and a practical necessity. Faith serves as the cornerstone for ambitious individuals, whether entrepreneurs, professionals, students, or dreamers. To nurture this foundational belief, setting clear intentions that align with one's core values becomes essential. When your actions resonate with what you fundamentally believe in, they foster an unwavering commitment to your vision. This alignment ensures that each decision, small or large, reinforces your dedication to achieving your dreams.

Imagine a student whose core value centers around innovation. To support his vision of becoming a leading technology expert, he sets specific intentions: pursuing relevant education, engaging in innovative projects, and consistently seeking new learning opportunities. These intentions act as a compass, guiding him even when faced with temptations or distractions. Clarity in intentions fosters a sense of purpose, ensuring that even during challenging times, there's a clear path forward steeped in personal conviction.

Beyond individual commitment, another critical strategy is building a supportive network. Surrounding oneself with like-minded individuals who believe in the same ideals can significantly impact one's ability to stay focused. A network provides emotional support, diverse perspectives, and constructive feedback, which are invaluable during setbacks. Picture an aspiring entrepreneur launching a startup: without a strong network, moments of doubt could derail progress. However, with mentors, collaborators, and fellow entrepreneurs to provide guidance and encouragement, resilience becomes a shared strength.

This collective resilience enables individuals to learn from their experiences rather than be deterred by them. For instance, a supportive network can offer insights on navigating market challenges, thereby turning potential failures into valuable lessons. Such a community helps maintain momentum towards fulfilling the vision, reinforcing belief through shared experiences and mutual growth.

Regularly visualizing success can also play a pivotal role in sustaining faith in one's vision. Visualization is not merely daydreaming; it's a proactive engagement with your goals that reaffirms belief and enhances motivation. When practiced consistently, visualization allows you to mentally rehearse every step toward reaching your milestones. Take, for example, a professional aiming to reach the top of their industry. By vividly imagining achieving this goal—feeling the sense of accomplishment, seeing themselves excel in their field—they bolster their confidence and heighten their drive.

Visualization empowers individuals to create a mental blueprint, offering clarity and focus amidst the inevitable chaos of daily life. It transforms abstract dreams into tangible objectives, making them feel more achievable. Moreover, it sharpens one's ability to identify opportunities and solutions that might otherwise go unnoticed, simply because the mind has been continually primed for success.

Another fundamental approach involves adopting a growth mindset. This concept, popularized by psychologist Carol Dweck, revolves around the belief that abilities and intelligence can be developed through dedication and hard work. Embracing a growth mindset encourages individuals to view failures not as endpoints but as stepping stones for personal development. When faith wavers due to setbacks, a growth mindset provides the assurance that with effort, learning, and persistence, success is still within reach.

Consider a dreamer who faces multiple rejections for a creative project. Instead of losing faith in their vision, they use these experiences as learning opportunities, adjusting strategies, refining skills, and gathering feedback to improve future outcomes. By viewing challenges as part of the growth process, faith in the ultimate vision remains intact. Each failure becomes a valuable lesson, reinforcing belief in their capability to succeed eventually.

Integrating these methods holistically creates a robust framework for developing and sustaining faith in one's vision. Each method complements the other, collectively fortifying belief and enabling individuals to navigate the ups and downs of their journeys. Setting clear intentions nurtures intrinsic motivation, while a supportive network offers external reinforcement. Regular visualization keeps motivation high, and a growth mindset ensures adaptability and resilience.

Final Insights

Belief is the cornerstone of transforming dreams into reality, a theme vividly illustrated in this chapter. Through examples such as Elon Musk's journey, we see how steadfast faith can lead to groundbreaking success despite significant challenges. His story exemplifies how belief, paired with determination and perseverance, can drive transformation on both personal and societal levels. The broader implications of having faith in one's vision suggest that it not only fuels individual progress but also inspires collective change.

The chapter also offers practical insights into cultivating and sustaining belief. Strategies like setting clear intentions, building a supportive network, practicing visualization, and adopting a growth mindset are crucial for maintaining motivation and resilience. These methods, when applied consistently, ensure that ambitious individuals from all walks of life remain engaged with their goals, turning perceived barriers into opportunities for growth. As readers reflect on these strategies, they are reminded of the power of belief in shaping paths toward success in today's ever-evolving world.

Chapter 4
Specialized Knowledge

Acquiring specialized knowledge is a key component in distinguishing oneself within any industry. It serves as a powerful tool that enables individuals to excel and stand out amidst the sea of general information that is widely accessible. In various fields, possessing unique skills and insights allows professionals to offer solutions and perspectives that are not only innovative but also invaluable. This chapter delves into the impact of specialized knowledge, how it shapes an individual's professional journey, and why it is more essential than ever in today's rapidly evolving world. The focus is on creating recognition and opening doors to unparalleled opportunities through expertise that is both rare and revered.

Readers will explore the numerous ways in which mastery in a specific domain can facilitate personal and professional advancements. From securing coveted positions that demand niche skills to navigating complex market challenges with confidence, the narrative unfolds with examples from diverse sectors, such as technology and healthcare. Additionally, this chapter discusses strategies for acquiring and honing specialized knowledge, including mentorship, continuous learning, and overcoming inherent obstacles. Each segment provides insights into aligning one's passion with their chosen field's demands, ultimately transforming aspirations into tangible success stories.

The Importance of Acquiring Specialized Knowledge

In today's dynamic world, where competition is fierce and industries are constantly evolving, possessing specialized knowledge has emerged as a crucial factor for personal and professional success. This form of knowledge allows individuals to distinguish themselves in their fields by offering unique skills and expertise that are rare or difficult to acquire. Imagine a landscape where everyone holds general knowledge; standing out becomes a challenge. However, specialized knowledge acts as a beacon, drawing attention and creating opportunities.

A prime example can be seen in the technology sector. With its rapid advancements, having a deep understanding of specific technologies or programming languages sets one apart from others. This expertise not only makes an individual valuable but also indispensable to employers who seek innovative solutions and fresh perspectives. By honing these specific skills, professionals gain a competitive advantage, ultimately leading to recognition and success within their industry.

Furthermore, in rapidly changing industries, possessing specialized knowledge is paramount for adapting to new challenges and innovations. The business environment today is marked by swift transformations driven by technological advancements, market demands, and global trends. Professionals with specialized knowledge can quickly adapt to these changes, leveraging their expertise to navigate uncharted territories effectively. For instance, individuals specializing in digital marketing can stay ahead by understanding the nuances of social media algorithms and online consumer behavior, enabling them to devise campaigns that yield optimal results even as platforms evolve.

In addition to adaptability, specialized knowledge fosters confidence and enhances decision-making abilities. When individuals have a comprehensive understanding of their field, they are more equipped to make informed decisions. This confidence stems from a deep-rooted familiarity with the subject matter, allowing them to evaluate situations critically and propose well-founded solutions. Consider a medical professional with specialized training in cardiology; their focused expertise empowers them to diagnose and treat complex cardiac conditions accurately, instilling trust and confidence in their patients.

Moreover, possessing specialized knowledge opens doors to better job opportunities and career advancement. In today's job market, certain roles demand specific expertise that cannot be fulfilled by generalists. Employers value specialists who can address niche needs and contribute uniquely to organizational goals. This demand often translates into lucrative positions and accelerated career growth. For example, professionals specializing in cybersecurity are increasingly sought after as organizations prioritize safeguarding their digital assets. Their unique skills ensure not only job security but also potential leadership roles as they guide companies in fortifying their defenses against cyber threats.

As we delve deeper into the significance of specialized knowledge, it's important to recognize its impact on personal development. Mastering a particular area requires dedication and continuous learning, fostering a sense of purpose and fulfillment. This journey of acquiring specialized knowledge encourages individuals to push boundaries, explore new insights, and remain engaged in their chosen field. The pursuit of expertise fuels creativity and innovation, driving both personal satisfaction and professional achievements.

For those aspiring to excel, embarking on the path to specialized knowledge involves identifying areas of interest and investing time and effort into mastering them. It's about finding that niche that resonates and aligning one's passion with the knowledge needed to thrive. Whether through formal education, practical experience, or self-driven learning, the process of gaining specialized knowledge offers a transformative journey, shaping not just careers but lives.

One highly effective approach to acquiring this knowledge is seeking mentorship from seasoned experts. Learning from those who have already navigated the complexities of a field provides invaluable insights and guidance. Experienced mentors can offer real-world perspectives, share lessons learned, and provide support as one embarks on their own journey toward specialization. Engaging with a community of like-minded individuals also enriches this process, offering diverse viewpoints and collaborative opportunities that further enhance one's expertise.

However, the pursuit of specialized knowledge is not without its challenges. It demands commitment, perseverance, and a willingness to embrace lifelong learning. As industries evolve, so too must one's understanding of their specialized area. Continuous education and staying abreast of developments are essential to maintaining relevance and maximizing opportunities for growth. Embracing change and proactively seeking new information ensures that specialized knowledge remains current and impactful.

Ultimately, the rewards of possessing specialized knowledge extend beyond professional achievements. It cultivates a mindset of curiosity and discovery, inspiring individuals to contribute meaningfully to their field and society at large. The influence of specialized knowledge ripples outward, sparking innovation and driving positive change across various sectors.

Case Study: Simone Biles—Mastering Gymnastics Through Relentless Learning and Practice

Simone Biles' journey to becoming one of the greatest gymnasts of all time is a compelling example of how specialized knowledge and dedicated practice can lead to exceptional success. Her story is not only about raw talent but also about an unwavering commitment to learning and refining her skills over countless hours of practice. From a young age, Biles showed an intrinsic interest in gymnastics, but what set her apart was her dedication to perfecting complex techniques. This devotion manifested in daily training sessions that often stretched for hours beyond regular practice times. Such relentless pursuit highlights the significance of consistent practice in mastering specialized knowledge.

Biles approached each routine as an opportunity to learn, meticulously analyzing every move, every landing, to identify where she could improve. This thoroughness in practicing and embracing feedback allowed her to build a robust foundation of skills that became second nature. Her repetitive drills might seem monotonous, yet they provided the precision needed to perform awe-inspiring routines under pressure. Consistent practice transformed potential into expertise, crafting a gymnast who wouldn't simply execute routines but innovate within them.

However, mastering complex techniques isn't without its challenges. Throughout her career, Biles faced setbacks, including injuries and disappointments in competitions. Yet, she exhibited remarkable resilience, viewing these obstacles not as failures but as lessons. Each challenge presented an opportunity to reassess, adapt, and return stronger. This mindset is crucial in skill acquisition, illustrating that achieving excellence requires not just hard work but also the ability to learn from every misstep. Biles' resilience taught her to trust in the process, understanding that progress is not always linear and that each setback is a stepping stone toward mastery.

Her resilience also played a pivotal role in fostering a growth mindset—a belief in the potential for development through effort and persistence. This perspective enabled Biles to continuously push her boundaries, ensuring she never settled for complacency. As she honed her craft, she developed a keen understanding of the sport's intricacies required for innovation. Biles wasn't content with merely participating; she sought to redefine what was possible in gymnastics. Her deep comprehension of the sport's physics and dynamics allowed her to introduce groundbreaking routines that challenged traditional norms.

An essential aspect of Biles' success was her curiosity and willingness to go beyond established routines. She often collaborated with coaches and experts, seeking their insights while contributing her ideas, leading to a creative synergy that birthed new moves previously unseen in the sport. This pursuit of innovation did not only enhance her performances but also cemented her legacy as a trailblazer, inspiring future generations of gymnasts to think creatively and explore uncharted territories within their disciplines.

Moreover, Biles' achievements underscore the need for passion as a driving force behind mastering any specialized field. Passion fuels the long hours of practice and sustains motivation during tough times, acting as a beacon that guides individuals through the complexities of their chosen pursuits. For Biles, gymnastics was not merely a sport but a vocation—a lifelong commitment that demanded perseverance, adaptability, and an insatiable desire to excel.

Her journey vividly demonstrates how specialized knowledge is built through intentional efforts that merge intellect, creativity, and determination. Whether it was the quiet hours spent rehearsing routines or the intense discussions with coaches on technique improvement, Biles' excellence emerged from a holistic approach to learning—one that integrated every aspect of her being toward reaching her goals.

In examining Simone Biles' path to greatness, we gain valuable insights into the principles underlying mastery: disciplined practice, resilience, deep understanding, innovation, and passion. Each element played a critical role in shaping her career, exemplifying how specialized knowledge is neither a gift nor an endpoint but an ongoing journey characterized by continuous learning and growth.

Through her triumphs and tribulations, Biles has become more than just a champion; she's a testament to what is possible when someone dedicates themselves entirely to their craft. In doing so, she offers a powerful narrative for anyone aspiring to achieve excellence in their respective fields. By embracing the tenets of hard work, resilience, and inventive thinking that defined Biles' trajectory, we, too, can transform our dreams into reality, uncovering new potentials as we navigate our paths.

Action Steps: Identifying Knowledge Gaps and Developing a Learning Plan

To excel in any field, understanding and filling your knowledge gaps is crucial. The first step in this journey is conducting a thorough self-assessment. This process allows you to pinpoint exactly where your current expertise might fall short in relation to your goals. Consider asking yourself questions such as: What skills do I currently possess? Which areas need improvement for me to reach my objectives? Use tools like skills inventories or reflective journaling to gain insights into your strengths and weaknesses. Identifying these gaps is the foundation for targeted learning and growth.

Once you have a clear picture of the areas needing enhancement, the next step is to create a structured learning plan. This plan should include specific objectives that are aligned with your personal or professional aspirations. For example, if you're aiming to master digital marketing, your objectives might involve understanding key concepts, using particular software, or developing analytical skills. Establish timelines for achieving each objective to maintain momentum and accountability. An effective learning plan also involves listing resources that can support your learning journey, whether it's books, online courses, or industry publications. Structure in learning ensures that every effort contributes meaningfully towards closing the identified knowledge gaps.

In pursuing knowledge, it's important to embrace a variety of learning methods. Traditional routes like attending workshops or enrolling in courses offer foundational knowledge and a structured environment. Meanwhile, mentoring provides a personalized approach, allowing you to gain insights from experienced individuals who have navigated paths similar to yours. Self-study, on the other hand, encourages independence and resourcefulness, letting you dive deeper into topics at your own pace. By combining these methods, you cater to different learning styles and needs, enriching your educational experience and gaining diverse perspectives.

As you strive to acquire new skills, regularly evaluating your progress is essential. This evaluation is not merely about keeping track of completed tasks but understanding how effectively your efforts translate into tangible growth. Are you meeting the timelines set out in your learning plan? Do you feel more confident in the areas you previously identified as weak? Reflecting on these questions allows you to measure your achievements against your initial objectives. It's vital to remain flexible; adjust your plan where necessary to accommodate changes in interest, market demands, or unforeseen challenges. Continuous growth requires adaptation—it's about making informed decisions to stay on course.

By combining self-awareness, structured planning, diverse learning strategies, and ongoing assessment, you build a robust framework for personal and professional advancement. This strategic approach not only helps fill knowledge gaps but also fosters a mindset geared towards lifelong learning. Each step you take in this direction enhances your capability to tackle challenges, innovate, and achieve success in your chosen field. Embrace this journey as an ongoing pursuit rather than a finite task, always seeking opportunities for learning and improvement along the way.

Start small and be patient with yourself. Recognize that acquiring specialized knowledge is a gradual process that demands time and persistence.

Acknowledge each milestone achieved and use these successes as motivation to continue pushing forward. As you progress, you not only enhance your existing skillset but also open doors to new opportunities that were previously beyond your reach.

Remember, the goal of identifying and filling knowledge gaps is not just about accumulating information but transforming it into confidence and competence. When you apply what you've learned effectively, you bolster both your professional value and personal satisfaction. Knowledge is a powerful tool when wielded with purpose, enabling you to make informed decisions and contribute meaningfully to your field.

Summary and Reflections

In this chapter, the focus has been on understanding the importance of acquiring specialized knowledge to excel in your chosen field. The examples and insights shared emphasize that having deep expertise can set you apart, making you an invaluable asset in today's competitive world. Through disciplines like technology, marketing, and cybersecurity, we see how specific skills lead to recognition, career growth, and the ability to navigate change with confidence. Simone Biles' story further illustrates how relentless practice and mastery of a particular craft can lead to remarkable achievements and redefine success. Her journey of dedication and resilience offers a powerful lesson in using specialized knowledge as a tool for innovation and empowerment.

As you consider your own aspirations, remember that embarking on this path involves identifying your interests and continuously learning to stay relevant. Creating a structured plan, seeking mentorship, and embracing diverse learning methods are crucial steps in building your skillset. By filling knowledge gaps with purpose, not only will you enhance your professional value but also discover new opportunities for personal fulfillment. This ongoing commitment to specialization drives both creativity and achievement, empowering you to reach new heights and make meaningful contributions to your field.

Chapter 5
Imagination as Your Workshop

Imagination serves as the foundation of innovation, acting as a limitless workshop where creativity and ideas blend to forge new paths toward wealth and success. This chapter explores how imagination fuels the ability to see potentials that others might overlook, enabling individuals to transform dreams into reality. The power of creative thinking is not just about coming up with new ideas but also about finding ways to implement them effectively in various contexts. By harnessing one's imaginative capabilities, individuals can navigate through challenges and embrace opportunities that lead to personal and financial growth.

In this chapter, we will delve into how creativity acts as a catalyst for generating novel solutions and driving economic value across different sectors. Readers will discover the importance of cultivating a mindset that fosters innovation, encouraging both risk-taking and resilience in the face of failure. Through various real-world examples and insights, the discussion highlights strategies for tapping into your creative potential, examining how environments rich in diversity and open collaboration can further enhance this process. Additionally, the chapter emphasizes understanding market dynamics to identify unmet needs and craft unique offerings accordingly, providing practical guidance on leveraging imagination as a critical tool for achieving ambitious goals in today's competitive landscape.

Ideas and Creativity: The Seeds of Wealth

In today's dynamic world, creativity and ideas serve as the bedrock for wealth creation. The ability to envision possibilities where none seem apparent is a powerful tool that can revolutionize industries. Take, for example, the transformation of entire sectors through the introduction of innovative products and services. These changes do not happen in isolation but are driven by individuals who dare to think differently.

Consider the impact of smart technology on our daily lives; the integration of smartphones has entirely altered communication methods and access to information. Transformative ideas like these have the capability to redefine market landscapes and create immense value. For entrepreneurs and innovators, the challenge lies in identifying opportunities where they can inject their unique insights, enabling them to stay ahead in competitive environments.

Creativity plays a critical role in problem-solving, often leading to groundbreaking solutions in business. When faced with seemingly insurmountable challenges, creative thinking allows individuals to approach problems from novel angles, uncovering paths that conventional thinking might overlook. This aspect is particularly important in business, where innovation is key to maintaining relevance and success. Companies that embrace creative problem-solving often find themselves at the forefront of their industries, capable of adapting swiftly to changing consumer needs and technological advancements.

Moreover, when we talk about wealth, it's essential to recognize that it's not confined to monetary gains alone. Wealth also encompasses intellectual property and brand value. Often, ideas cultivated into patents or trademarks become lucrative assets, offering long-term revenue streams while simultaneously enhancing company prestige. Such intellectual properties not only contribute financially but also fortify a company's position in the market, acting as barriers against competition.

Successful innovators possess an acute ability to identify unmet needs and address them through creative solutions. This skill requires both intuition and a deep understanding of market dynamics. By observing gaps in existing markets or predicting future demands, innovators can tailor their offerings to meet those specific requirements. This practice involves more than just luck; it requires diligent research, empathy towards consumer experiences, and relentless experimentation.

The journey of recognizing these unmet needs starts with thorough market analysis, where trends and patterns offer clues about potential areas for growth. Innovators employ design thinking—a process that places the consumer at the heart of the solution development—to generate practical and appealing products. With this approach, companies not only fulfill current consumer expectations but also anticipate future desires, which is crucial for sustained success.

While discussing creativity's critical role in wealth creation, it's important to acknowledge the environment that fosters such innovative thinking. A culture encouraging experimentation without fear of failure can significantly enhance the potential for groundbreaking discoveries. Organizations that cultivate an atmosphere of open dialogue and collaboration often find themselves thriving with fresh ideas and perspectives.

Fostering such an environment often means embracing diversity in thought and experience. Different perspectives invite broader considerations, bringing together varied approaches to tackling challenges. It is in these heterogeneous settings that creativity reaches its full potential, leading to richer, more robust solutions.

Furthermore, investing in creativity training and idea generation workshops can bolster an organization's ability to innovate continuously. These initiatives teach teams how to unlock their latent creative potential and apply it effectively toward real-world challenges. Cultivating these skills across all levels ensures that creativity is embedded within the organizational fabric, not just isolated within specific departments.

In essence, the interplay between creativity and ideas is profound. It catalyzes industry shifts, drives solutions to complex problems, expands the definition of wealth beyond mere dollars, and equips innovators to address emerging market needs creatively. For ambitious individuals seeking personal and financial success, harnessing the power of imagination is not just advantageous—it is imperative. They must embrace a mindset that values curiosity, encourages exploration, and nurtures originality as vital components of achieving their grand visions.

Case Study: Reed Hastings and Netflix

Reed Hastings' innovative approach to building Netflix offers an insightful look into harnessing creativity to disrupt established norms. Initially launched as a DVD rental-by-mail service, Netflix under Hastings' leadership soon grew to challenge traditional media. By embracing the burgeoning digital landscape, Netflix offered on-demand streaming services that completely redefined how audiences consumed content. This was a bold move during a time when the majority of entertainment consumption happened via cable television and movie theaters. Hastings foresaw the potential for digital streaming to revolutionize the industry, demonstrating the power of seeing beyond conventional models.

His willingness to rethink entertainment consumption played a pivotal role in Netflix's global success. The idea of binge-watching—consuming multiple episodes or even entire seasons in one sitting—emerged from this new model. Hastings recognized that audiences craved more flexibility and freedom in how they engaged with media. Streaming gave viewers unprecedented control over what they watched and when, breaking away from fixed programming schedules and appealing to the modern consumer's desire for instant gratification. This radical shift not only catered to audience preferences but also influenced competitors to reconsider their own strategies, reinforcing the importance of being adaptable and forward-thinking in business.

One of the key differentiating factors that set Netflix apart was its emphasis on user experience and personalized content. From the onset, Hastings prioritized creating a platform that was intuitive and easy to navigate. Understanding that user satisfaction was paramount, Netflix invested heavily in technology to track viewing habits and preferences. This data-driven approach allowed the company to deliver personalized recommendations, enhancing user engagement and loyalty. The algorithms developed by Netflix are now seen as benchmarks for personalization in digital platforms, underscoring how technological innovation can enhance product offerings and create a competitive edge.

The commitment to continuous adaptation is another hallmark of Hastings' strategy. In a rapidly changing entertainment landscape, resting on past successes was never an option. Anticipating shifts in viewer behavior, Netflix made a substantial investment in original content, producing acclaimed series like "Stranger Things" and "The Crown". By doing so, Netflix not only differentiated itself from other streaming services that relied solely on licensed content but also asserted creative control over its offerings. Original content served as both a unique selling point and a way to attract diverse global audiences, establishing Netflix as a formidable player in international markets.

Furthermore, Hastings' ability to envision Netflix as more than just a streaming service was crucial for its sustained growth. By venturing into production and becoming a major studio in its own right, Netflix ensured it had a continuous pipeline of exclusive hits that kept subscribers engaged. This diversification reduced dependency on third-party content and mitigated risks associated with expiring licenses that had previously impacted the availability of popular shows on the platform. Through strategic partnerships and acquisitions, Netflix maintained its relevance in an industry characterized by fierce competition and rapid technological advancements.

To fully appreciate the narrative of Netflix's rise, it is important to consider the broader context of the media landscape at the time. Traditional media companies were typically slow to embrace new technologies, constrained by legacy systems and existing content distribution contracts. This environment provided Hastings the opening he needed to capitalize on emerging trends. His ability to anticipate market demands and adapt technological innovations effectively reshaped consumer expectations. Moreover, Netflix's global expansion strategy mirrored Hastings' commitment to growth, demonstrating how thinking beyond geographical boundaries could significantly broaden market reach.

Hastings' journey with Netflix exemplifies the transformative power of imagination in business. Through his vision, he showcased how challenging the status quo could lead to unparalleled success. Entrepreneurs aiming for personal and financial achievements can draw lessons from Hastings' story, particularly the value of innovation, user-centricity, and adaptability in pursuing ambitious goals. This narrative underscores the profound impact that daring to think differently can have on overcoming entrenched barriers in any industry.

An interesting exercise to help foster similar innovation is to engage in regular brainstorming sessions. Allowing teams within a company to explore various ideas without immediate judgment can spark creativity and lead to unique solutions. Similarly, designing a vision board can aid in goal setting, providing a visual representation of aims and inspiring action towards achieving them. Both practices encourage ongoing ideation and reflection, which are essential components for sustaining innovation and adapting to evolving markets.

Brainstorming: A Tool for Innovation

In the domain of creativity and innovation, brainstorming stands out as a vital tool. It serves not only as a workshop for ideas but also as a platform where judgment is suspended in favor of open collaboration. In today's fast-paced world, where the ability to innovate can distinguish between success and stagnation, brainstorming becomes indispensable. It invites people to share their thoughts freely, fostering an environment that encourages wild ideas and unexpected solutions. This practice is crucial for ambitious individuals who are reaching for personal and financial success.

At its core, brainstorming is about collaborative idea generation. This process thrives on diversity, bringing together people with different backgrounds, perspectives, and expertise. Each participant contributes unique insights, collectively forming a pool of potential creative solutions. For example, in a team developing a new app, one member might suggest a feature inspired by social media trends, while another proposes technical improvements based on user data. By welcoming all contributions, no matter how unpolished or unconventional, teams build a rich tapestry of possibilities that a solitary effort might not achieve.

Think of brainstorming as a stimulant for creative thinking. It unlocks latent potential within individuals and teams alike. Often, we have hidden reservoirs of creativity that remain untapped simply because we haven't applied them in a conducive setting. Brainstorming sessions create such an environment, acting like a catalyst that speeds up the reaction of generating novel ideas. Consider the context of a marketing firm tasked with launching a groundbreaking campaign. Here, brainstorming could reveal an array of concepts ranging from leveraging viral content strategies to identifying niche market segments previously overlooked.

Moreover, the diverse perspectives brought forward during brainstorming sessions lead to more comprehensive solutions. A multifaceted approach considers various angles and possibilities, enhancing the depth of exploration beyond conventional thinking. When engaging voices from different sectors in a business meeting, for instance, a product development plan may benefit from insights related to customer service, logistics, and user experience design. This blend of viewpoints ultimately results in a strategic advantage, ensuring that all aspects of a problem are scrutinized and addressed.

Regularly practicing brainstorming enhances flexibility and adaptability in problem-solving. Like any skill, creativity improves with use. As individuals become accustomed to generating and evaluating ideas, their ability to shift gears in response to new challenges strengthens. This adaptability is crucial in environments that require constant evolution and responsiveness, such as technology startups or creative agencies. Teams who regularly engage in brainstorming find themselves better prepared to pivot when faced with unforeseen obstacles or market changes.

While brainstorming is often associated with group settings, solo brainstorming should not be overlooked. Individuals can benefit immensely from setting aside dedicated time to explore ideas independently, free from external constraints or influences. This practice can complement group sessions, providing clearer personal insights that contribute to collective discussions. Importantly, whether performed alone or in groups, the key is maintaining an open-minded approach that prioritizes idea-generation over critique at initial stages.

To further enhance the effectiveness of brainstorming, it's beneficial to establish some simple guidelines. These include encouraging participation from everyone, avoiding criticism during idea generation, and building on each other's suggestions. It may also help to set a time limit to prevent discussions from meandering and to keep the energy levels high. Notably, tools like mind maps or digital brainstorming applications can facilitate the organization and visualization of ideas, making it easier to spot connections and patterns that might otherwise be missed.

Vision Boards: Visualizing Success

Imagination is not just a flight of fancy; it serves as a critical tool in our personal workshop for crafting success. One powerful way to harness imagination is through the creation of vision boards. Vision boards bring clarity to our goals and aspirations by providing a tangible reminder of them, transforming abstract dreams into concrete targets. By assembling images that reflect your desires—whether it's a dream home, an ultimate career goal, or a significant life milestone—you create a visual snapshot of where you want to go.

The act of selecting and arranging images on a board invigorates your motivation. This process is about connecting with your innermost dreams and bringing them to life in a visual format that can ignite passion and determination. For instance, if your ambition is to travel the world, seeing images of iconic landmarks daily will reinforce this goal in your subconscious mind, encouraging you to take actionable steps towards achieving it.

Including specific images on your vision board works like a laser focus for your efforts. Vague goals are often difficult to pursue, as they lack direction. However, when you include definite pictures, symbols, or words that directly relate to your objectives, you give form and detail to your ambitions. For example, instead of merely envisioning "success," picture yourself receiving an award in your career field or imagine the joy of opening your own business. Specificity allows you to delineate the path needed to reach these outcomes.

Vision boards do more than just inspire; they clarify intentions. When you look at your board regularly, it becomes easier to identify what truly matters to you and what steps need to be taken next. This clarity can strip away distractions, helping to focus both your conscious and subconscious actions toward your end game. The clearer the image of what you want to achieve, the more straightforward it becomes to develop strategies and plans to get there.

Moreover, maintaining momentum is crucial in any journey toward success. Just as athletes continuously train to stay in peak condition, reviewing and updating your vision board keeps your goals fresh and your determination strong. Life evolves, and so should your vision board. As goals are met or change, adjusting the board to reflect new ambitions is essential. This ongoing process acknowledges progress and helps sustain motivation over time.

Regularly engaging with your vision board also fosters a sense of accountability. It acts as a checkpoint—a reflective surface showing where you currently stand versus where you aspire to be. This honest reckoning can spur critical self-reflection, prompting adjustments in strategy or mindset when necessary. Seeing potential roadblocks alongside your goals allows you to plan preemptively, positioning yourself better to handle challenges along the way.

Furthermore, the emotional connection created by a vision board cannot be understated. Emotions play a significant role in shaping our behaviors and choices. By tapping into feelings of excitement, anticipation, and joy that arise from seeing your ideal future represented visually, you create an emotional resonance that fuels perseverance. These feelings become powerful catalysts, pushing you to step outside your comfort zone and try new things.

For ambitious individuals, the practice of using vision boards is a dynamic and evolving process. It doesn't just empower personal growth but also enhances professional development. Entrepreneurs and professionals alike can benefit from turning their business dreams into detailed visual narratives, fostering innovation and driving forward-thinking strategies.

For students and dreamers, a vision board can transform vague educational and career aspirations into coherent, achievable goals. Students might incorporate images of prestigious universities, coveted internships, or inspirational figures in their fields of interest, which serve as constant reminders of their academic and professional targets.

In essence, a vision board is more than a collection of images; it is a strategic blueprint for how you wish to build your life. Discipline in creating, updating, and interacting with your board can translate abstract dreams into tangible reality. It's a tool that bridges the gap between vision and realization, offering direction and reinforcing commitment.

Concluding Thoughts

Throughout this chapter, we explored the significant role creativity and ideas play in fostering wealth and driving innovation. By examining how creative thought can solve problems and reveal new opportunities, we've seen how individuals and companies alike can achieve remarkable success.

Take the example of transformative technologies like smart devices; they have changed how we live and work by presenting possibilities previously unseen. We also looked at how businesses that embrace creativity thrive by staying ahead of ever-evolving consumer needs. The chapter demonstrated that wealth isn't just measured in money; it includes intellectual assets like patents and brand value, which serve as long-term benefits ensuring a company's competitive edge.

Furthermore, Reed Hastings' journey with Netflix exemplified how bold, innovative thinking could challenge industry norms and lead to profound business outcomes. His story highlighted the importance of being adaptable and user-focused in today's fast-changing landscape. From brainstorming sessions to vision boards, tools for enhancing creativity were discussed, showing their utility in turning dreams into achievable goals. Ultimately, this chapter underlined the power of imagination as a crucial element for ambitious individuals seeking personal and financial growth. By nurturing a mindset that values curiosity and encourages exploration, you can open doors to both personal fulfillment and professional success.

Chapter 6
Organized Planning

Organized planning is all about turning a vision into actionable steps. As many can attest, having a dream is just the beginning. The real challenge lies in mapping out how to achieve that dream. Planning transforms abstract ideas into a structured sequence of actions, bringing clarity and direction to ambitions. By establishing a detailed plan, individuals can focus their energy on specific objectives, making the path forward more navigable and less overwhelming. This approach ensures that every effort contributes meaningfully towards reaching the desired outcome, creating a bridge between aspiration and achievement.

This chapter delves into the essential elements required for organized planning. Readers will explore methods to create a strategic outline, breaking down broad visions into smaller, attainable goals. Discover how feedback loops are instrumental in keeping plans relevant amidst changing conditions and how crucial alignment is in ensuring everyone involved shares a united goal.

The chapter further examines practical steps like defining the vision clearly, setting deadlines, and fostering team cooperation. Throughout these discussions, the aim is to equip ambitious individuals with tools to transform their ideas into reality, maintaining momentum and overcoming challenges along the way.

Vision to Action

A visionary idea is the spark that ignites ambition and fuels innovation. However, without a plan to guide its realization, even the most brilliant vision can flounder. The first step in transforming a visionary idea into an actionable plan is recognizing the importance of a clear, compelling vision as the backbone of all planning activities. This vision serves as both the starting point and the north star, guiding every decision and action taken towards fulfilling the overarching goals.

Developing a structured outline is crucial in breaking down broad visions into specific, achievable objectives. This process involves dissecting the grand idea into manageable components, each with its own set of goals and milestones. Think of it as creating a roadmap where each stop represents a smaller objective that, when reached, brings you closer to the ultimate destination. For instance, if the vision is to revolutionize an industry, initial objectives might include conducting market research, developing a prototype, and securing initial funding. By focusing on these smaller steps, the path forward becomes less daunting and more actionable.

Feedback loops play a vital role in refining and adjusting plans to keep them relevant and responsive to changing circumstances. These loops involve regularly reviewing progress, gathering input from various stakeholders, and making necessary adjustments to the plan. Consider them checkpoints where insights and feedback are gathered to ensure the project is on track. An example of this in practice could be a tech startup that routinely gathers user feedback during beta testing phases. Such information can be invaluable, allowing the team to pivot or enhance features in alignment with customer needs and market trends.

Ensuring alignment across teams and stakeholders is essential for maintaining cohesive progress toward the vision. When everyone involved understands and embraces the vision, they are more likely to work collaboratively toward common goals. Alignment can be fostered through regular communication, transparency about objectives and progress, and involving key players in decision-making processes. This not only builds trust but also harnesses collective expertise and creativity. Imagine a marketing team and a product development team working together seamlessly; their aligned efforts result in a product launch that not only meets internal benchmarks but also resonates well with consumers.

To transform a visionary idea into an actionable plan effectively, a few action steps can be followed:

1. **Define the Vision** : Clearly articulate what the end goal looks like. Make sure this vision is inspiring yet attainable, serving as motivation for all parties involved.
1. **Break It Down** : Develop a detailed outline by dividing the vision into smaller, reachable objectives. Assign timelines and responsibilities to each task to maintain focus and momentum.
1. **Establish Feedback Mechanisms** : Set up regular intervals for review and feedback. Encourage open communication among team members and adapt plans based on new insights or shifts in the landscape.
1. **Foster Team Alignment** : Hold regular meetings to ensure everyone is on the same

page. Communicate openly about the vision and how each individual's contributions fit into the bigger picture.

Strategic Planning at Facebook

Sheryl Sandberg's impact on Facebook is a prime example of the power of strategic planning. When she joined Facebook as Chief Operating Officer, the company was on the brink of rapid evolution. Sandberg played a crucial role in orchestrating the company's exponential growth by implementing a comprehensive framework that would steer Facebook to new heights. Her approach was built on a foundation of strategic clarity and determined execution.

Sandberg's method was to develop and execute strategic plans that directly addressed both immediate needs and future aspirations. She understood that for Facebook to grow at such an impressive pace, it needed a well-structured roadmap that allowed for dynamic progress while also keeping an eye on long-term objectives. This strategic planning became evident when Facebook underwent significant expansion phases, including its initial public offering (IPO) and global diversification efforts.

One of Sandberg's key contributions was her ability to organize goals effectively across different levels of the organization. She embraced a tiered approach that tackled both short-term obstacles and long-term vision simultaneously. By doing so, Sandberg ensured that every team within Facebook had a clear understanding of their objectives and how they fit into the broader company mission. This clear alignment helped Facebook effectively navigate challenges as they emerged, whether they were related to technological advancements or market competition.

A significant aspect of Sandberg's strategy was her emphasis on the coordination of cross-functional teams. At Facebook, collaboration across various domains such as engineering, marketing, and product development was essential for unified operation. Sandberg championed an environment where open communication was encouraged, enabling different teams to work together toward common goals. This not only streamlined processes but also fostered innovation through diverse perspectives.

The success of these coordinated efforts can be attributed to Sandberg's knack for bringing together teams with varying expertise to solve complex problems. Under her guidance, Facebook executed sophisticated projects like integrating new features and expanding advertising capabilities, all while maintaining a seamless user experience. The coordinated approach reduced operational silos and paved the way for a synchronized execution of the company's strategic plans.

Another key element of Sandberg's tenure at Facebook was her advocacy for adaptive strategies. In the fast-evolving tech landscape, sticking rigidly to predetermined plans can lead to stagnation. Sandberg recognized this and advocated for flexibility in planning. She promoted a culture where teams were encouraged to adapt strategies based on real-time data, feedback, and emerging trends. This adaptability was crucial in allowing Facebook to remain at the forefront of innovation and stay competitive in the tech industry.

Facebook's ability to quickly pivot and innovate under Sandberg's leadership is a testament to the effectiveness of adopting adaptive strategies. For instance, when faced with privacy concerns and regulatory challenges, Facebook swiftly adjusted its policies and products to meet new standards while still pursuing growth opportunities. This agility showcased how strategic planning could enable a company to be resilient amid uncertainty.

In evaluating Sandberg's influence on Facebook's journey, it becomes apparent that her strategic planning was instrumental in propelling the company forward. Her focus on immediate priorities and long-term ambitions created a balanced approach that responded to internal and external pressures. Through effective goal-setting, cross-functional teamwork, and adaptive strategies, Sandberg carved out a model of planning that transformed Facebook from a burgeoning social network into a global powerhouse.

Breaking Down Long-Term Goals

When setting out to achieve expansive, long-term goals, the challenge often lies in breaking down these mammoth tasks into smaller, manageable steps. This can transform a daunting vision into a series of achievable tasks that build momentum and sustain progress over time. Imagine an entrepreneur with the ambition to expand their business internationally. The initial goal may seem overwhelming, but by dividing it into smaller objectives, such as researching target markets, securing funding, and developing export strategies, each step becomes more attainable and less intimidating. Setting realistic deadlines for these tasks is crucial. Without clear timelines, even the most well-intentioned plans can falter or lose direction. Deadlines act as both motivators and checkpoints, helping individuals gauge whether they are on track or if adjustments are needed.

Once tasks are broken down, prioritizing them based on urgency and importance can maximize efficiency. This means recognizing which tasks will have the most significant impact on the overall goal and addressing them first. Often, this involves distinguishing between what needs immediate attention and what can wait—a skill that can boost productivity significantly. For example, prioritizing market research before product development ensures resources are allocated wisely and that the final offering truly meets consumer needs. Techniques such as Eisenhower's Urgent-Important Matrix can be invaluable here, aiding in differentiating critical tasks from distractions, thus ensuring focus remains on high-impact activities.

The allocation of resources also plays a pivotal role in planning effectively for long-term goals. Adequate distribution of time, finances, and human capital across various stages of goal achievement can prevent bottlenecks and inefficiencies. Consider a student striving to graduate with honors. Allocating appropriate study time, seeking mentorship, and balancing extracurricular activities throughout their education journey requires careful planning and smart resource distribution. This might involve budgeting time for intensive exam preparations or securing necessary materials well in advance to avoid last-minute pressures.

Tracking progress throughout this journey is equally essential. Utilizing progress-tracking tools helps measure ongoing success and allows for timely adjustments. Whether it's software applications or simple spreadsheets, these tools provide valuable insights into how closely one's actions align with set objectives. With digital tools, entrepreneurs can monitor sales growth, customer engagement, or project milestones, enabling them to make informed decisions about future directions. Moreover, seeing tangible progress can be incredibly motivating and reinforce commitment to the larger goal. Regularly reviewing these metrics offers the opportunity to celebrate small wins and recalibrate plans as needed, maintaining a steady course toward the ultimate objective.

Actionable Steps and Deadlines

In the realm of organized planning, transforming lofty visions into tangible achievements is both an art and a science. For those seeking personal or financial success, mastering this transformation process is crucial. A critical step is establishing concrete actions tied to deadlines, which forms the backbone of any effective execution plan.

To begin with, setting specific milestones that are time-bound is indispensable for ensuring accountability. Imagine embarking on a journey without knowing your destination or the stops along the way—this would lead to confusion and inefficiency. Similarly, defining clear milestones acts as checkpoints that guide progress and provide structure. Each milestone should serve a purpose, offering measurable targets that can be evaluated and adjusted if necessary. This approach not only clarifies expectations but also motivates individuals as they achieve each small victory on the path to the ultimate goal.

Next, adopting project management methodologies can greatly enhance the organization of tasks and adherence to schedules. Tools such as Gantt charts, Kanban boards, or Agile frameworks can help break down complex projects into manageable parts. By visualizing tasks, tracking progress, and identifying dependencies, these methodologies streamline processes and facilitate smoother operations. An entrepreneur, for instance, might utilize these tools to coordinate product development phases, ensuring timely completion while accommodating changes swiftly. These techniques empower planners to allocate resources efficiently and prioritize tasks effectively, leading to optimized results.

However, no plan is immune to challenges. Identifying potential obstacles before they arise is vital for maintaining momentum. Developing contingency plans can mitigate risks and protect against derailments. Consider a team working on launching a new software product. They might anticipate issues like technological constraints or market shifts. By having backup strategies in place, such as alternative suppliers or flexible marketing strategies, they can shift gears quickly without losing significant time or resources. This foresightedness means being proactive rather than reactive, allowing teams to adapt while keeping the overall plan intact.

Regular meetings and check-ins play a pivotal role in keeping everyone informed and aligned with the project's objectives. Communication is the glue that holds teams together, especially when working toward a common goal. Scheduled meetings create opportunities for team members to share updates, address concerns, and celebrate achievements, fostering a sense of community and shared purpose. Moreover, these sessions offer platforms for problem-solving through collaborative efforts, often resulting in innovative solutions that might not emerge in isolation. For example, a company undergoing organizational change may benefit from weekly status updates that ensure transparency and boost morale by involving all stakeholders in decision-making processes.

Creating systems for accountability further strengthens the foundation of any organized plan. Accountability drives responsibility and commitment among team members. Implementing evaluation metrics allows for the assessment of individual and group performance relative to defined goals. By recognizing achievements—and identifying areas needing improvement—teams maintain focus and motivation. It's important to recognize that accountability is not about placing blame but rather encouraging progress and learning. In this context, feedback becomes a tool for growth, helping participants refine their approaches and enhance their skills.

Effective use of technology significantly contributes to efficient plan execution. Software tools designed for task management, like Trello or Asana, simplify assigning responsibilities and tracking progress. These platforms offer real-time insights into project developments, enabling quick adjustments and better collaboration across dispersed teams. In today's digital age, leveraging such technology reduces miscommunications and speeds up decision-making, ultimately supporting the successful completion of planned activities.

Furthermore, the power of delegation cannot be underestimated in achieving organized planning. Delegation involves assigning appropriate responsibilities to individuals based on their strengths and expertise. It not only empowers team members but also prevents burnout among leaders who may otherwise become overwhelmed by managing every detail. Trusting team members to handle specific tasks promotes a culture of ownership and accountability, enhancing collective efficiency and drive towards common objectives.

Lastly, reflection and reevaluation are integral components of sustaining organized planning. Regularly reviewing progress against established benchmarks allows for adjustments that respond to evolving circumstances. This adaptability is essential in navigating the unpredictable nature of business and personal projects. Through honest assessments, teams can recalibrate strategies to remain aligned with the overarching vision, incorporating lessons learned into future planning endeavors.

Bringing It All Together

In this chapter, the focus has been on transforming visionary ideas into actionable plans through strategic and detailed planning. It explored how a compelling vision acts as both a guiding force and an inspiration, necessary for mapping out the journey toward achieving one's goals. By breaking down ambitious visions into smaller, manageable tasks, individuals and teams can maintain momentum and make steady progress. The importance of feedback loops was highlighted as well, serving to continually refine strategies in response to new insights and circumstances. This ensures that the plan remains aligned with evolving needs and objectives, allowing for effective adaptation.

Moreover, ensuring alignment across various stakeholders is crucial for cohesive progress.

Regular communication and transparency help build trust and foster collaboration among teams, making collective efforts towards a common goal more efficient and innovative. Practical steps such as setting clear milestones with deadlines, adopting project management tools, and promoting accountability were discussed as vital components in this process. By utilizing these strategies, individuals aiming for personal or financial success can effectively turn their visions into reality, navigating challenges with agility and foresight.

Chapter 7
The Mastermind Alliance

Forming a mastermind alliance is the key to unlocking personal and professional growth. The idea revolves around bringing together a group of individuals who possess diverse skills, knowledge, and experiences, aimed at achieving greater successes collectively than one could alone. Imagine the dynamic possibilities when minds unite, sharing ideas, offering support, and challenging each other to reach higher goals. This network of collaboration cultivates an environment conducive to innovation and problem-solving, capitalizing on the strengths of each member and fostering a culture where mutual encouragement propels everyone forward.

In this chapter, we delve into the essence of why surrounding oneself with a supportive and knowledgeable team is vital for success. Readers will explore how such alliances can inspire emotional resilience during challenging times and offer a reservoir of expertise accessible to all members. We'll discuss the profound impact of accountability within these groups, highlighting how it drives individuals toward achieving their objectives. Further examination reveals how mastermind alliances promote personal development and decision-making synergy through diverse perspectives. By engaging with this chapter, you'll gain insights into forming your own powerful coalition of mentors and collaborators, ultimately enhancing both personal satisfaction and career advancement.

The Power of Supportive Teams

Understanding the impact of having a supportive team is crucial for personal and professional success. When individuals come together to form a cohesive unit, they create an environment ripe for innovation and progress. This collaborative energy arises primarily from the diverse perspectives that each member brings to the table. Every person in a team has unique experiences and insights, which can lead to creative problem-solving and novel solutions. For example, consider a tech startup where engineers, designers, and marketers work side by side. The engineers might focus on functionality, while designers concentrate on aesthetics, and marketers emphasize user engagement. When these viewpoints intertwine, the result is often a groundbreaking product that appeals to a broad audience.

Beyond fostering innovation, a supportive team plays a significant role in bolstering emotional resilience. Life's challenges can be daunting when faced alone, but with a group of peers providing encouragement and empathy, individuals are better equipped to tackle obstacles. Imagine an entrepreneur who faces setbacks during the launch of a new venture. With a team offering reassurance and constructive feedback, the entrepreneur can regain motivation and maintain focus. This emotional fortitude not only enhances productivity but also instills a sense of belonging and camaraderie among team members.

Another invaluable benefit of being part of a supportive team is access to a wealth of resources and information. A network of knowledgeable individuals serves as a vast reservoir of expertise, offering insights and advice that can propel one's growth. Consider a professional seeking to advance in their career. By being part of a mastermind group, this individual can tap into the experiences of others who have navigated similar paths. Through shared knowledge, they gain access to new strategies and tools, enabling them to make informed decisions and achieve their goals more efficiently.

Moreover, the presence of a supportive team encourages accountability, driving higher goal achievement. When individuals commit to a common purpose within a mastermind alliance, they feel responsible not only to themselves but also to their peers. Regular check-ins and shared progress updates ensure that everyone stays on track and remains committed to their objectives. Take, for instance, a group of writers working on separate projects. By holding each other accountable through weekly meetings, they push one another to meet deadlines and produce high-quality work. This accountability fosters a culture of diligence and determination, ultimately leading to greater success for each member.

Inclusion in a mastermind group goes beyond mere goal-setting; it nurtures personal development and self-awareness. Engaging with a diverse set of individuals allows for continuous learning and reflection. Members are challenged to question their assumptions and broaden their horizons, leading to personal growth. For instance, a business leader might gain new perspectives on leadership styles by interacting with peers from different industries. These interactions spark introspection, prompting the leader to refine their approach and adapt to changing circumstances.

Furthermore, the synergy created by a supportive team enhances decision-making processes. When faced with critical choices, having a group to brainstorm with ensures that all angles are considered. Collaborative discussions often uncover potential pitfalls and alternative solutions that might be overlooked by an individual. Picture a nonprofit organization strategizing on how to maximize its impact. By leveraging the collective wisdom of its board members, the organization can devise comprehensive plans that address various stakeholder needs. This thoroughness leads to more effective outcomes and long-term sustainability.

Lastly, being part of a supportive team contributes to an individual's overall well-being. The companionship and understanding offered by fellow members alleviate stress and build psychological resilience. During trying times, knowing that one is not alone provides comfort and hope. Imagine a student navigating the pressures of academic life. With a study group offering support, the student gains confidence and feels empowered to face challenges. This positive reinforcement not only boosts academic performance but also nurtures a sense of fulfillment and happiness.

Case Study: Steve Jobs and Steve Wozniak

In the story of Apple's meteoric rise, the collaboration between Steve Jobs and Steve Wozniak stands out as a prime example of how diverse talents can combine to achieve phenomenal success. The partnership was a blend of artful vision and technical mastery, illustrating how two different minds came together to forge something extraordinary.

Steve Jobs was the quintessential visionary leader. His unparalleled ability to foresee the future of personal computing, paired with his knack for marketing, paved the way for Apple's brand to become iconic. Jobs had an innate talent for understanding what consumers wanted before they even knew it themselves. He could distill complex technological ideas into compelling narratives that captured the public's imagination. This skill set was a crucial driver in creating a memorable brand image and fostering consumer desire for Apple's products.

On the other hand, Steve Wozniak brought unmatched technical prowess to the table. Known affectionately as "Woz," he was the engineering mastermind behind Apple's early hardware innovations. Where Jobs saw potential, Wozniak saw solutions—he was the architect who translated vision into reality. His creativity and deep understanding of electronics allowed him to design revolutionary products like the Apple I and Apple II computers. These machines were not just technical marvels; they were user-friendly, setting new standards in the tech industry.

The synergy between Jobs and Wozniak was evident in their complementary roles. Jobs' leadership provided the framework and vision around which Apple could grow, while Wozniak's technical expertise filled in the necessary details to make it all possible. Their collaboration exemplifies how blending distinct skills can lead to groundbreaking innovation. Each brought strengths that covered the other's weaknesses, forming a well-rounded team capable of realizing ambitious goals that seemed unattainable on their own.

Their combined efforts led to efficient problem-solving and rapid product development. Jobs had a relentless drive for perfection, pushing the boundaries of what was possible both aesthetically and functionally. His insistence on quality often pushed Wozniak to innovate beyond conventional limits, leading to faster development cycles and superior products. This dynamic relationship fostered an environment where challenges became opportunities for creative problem-solving rather than obstacles.

One notable instance of their collaborative synergy occurred during the development of the Apple II. While Wozniak was focused on refining the circuitry and enhancing performance, Jobs concentrated on the design aesthetics and usability features. This dual focus ensured that the Apple II was not only powerful but also appealing to the average consumer, thereby expanding its reach and marketability. It demonstrated how their partnership was more than the sum of its parts, elevating the product's impact in the marketplace.

Furthermore, this case underscores the importance of aligning complementary strengths within a team. By combining their unique talents, Jobs and Wozniak created a powerful alliance that propelled Apple from a small garage operation into a global technology leader. Their example highlights the benefits of assembling a team where varied expertise is harnessed towards a unified goal. In any industry, aligning different strengths allows a group to tackle challenges from multiple angles, increasing the chance of innovative outcomes.

The lessons learned from Jobs and Wozniak's partnership remain relevant today. For individuals and organizations alike, the key takeaway is that no one person has all the answers. Success often comes from recognizing one's limitations and seeking partners whose skills complement your own. By doing so, you create a robust network capable of weathering adversity and seizing opportunities.

While the dynamic between Jobs and Wozniak was specific to its time and context, the principles behind their collaboration are timeless. Visionary leadership must be balanced with expert execution, and creativity should work hand-in-hand with practicality. When these elements function in harmony, remarkable achievements are within reach.

Identifying Potential Mentors and Collaborators

To harness the power of a mastermind alliance, it's crucial to start by understanding your personal and professional aspirations. Begin by reflecting on what you truly want to achieve and where you might lack the necessary expertise. This introspective step is vital as it helps pinpoint specific areas where external input could accelerate your progress. Whether you're aiming for business growth, career advancement, or personal development, identifying these gaps will guide you in seeking out individuals whose strengths complement your needs.

Once you've clarified your goals, consider attending networking events and industry conferences. These gatherings are fertile ground for meeting potential collaborators who share your interests or have experience in areas you wish to explore. Being in an environment where knowledge exchange is encouraged can lead to fruitful connections. For example, engaging in conversations during panel discussions or social gatherings at these events opens doors to new opportunities and ideas. By actively participating, you position yourself to connect with like-minded individuals who value collaboration and innovation.

In today's digital age, online platforms like LinkedIn offer vast opportunities to expand your professional network beyond geographical limitations. By optimizing your profile with detailed information about your skills, achievements, and aspirations, you make it easier for others to find and engage with you. LinkedIn isn't just a platform for job searches; it's a community where professionals from various fields converge, discuss trends, and share insights. Participate in groups, join discussions, and reach out to individuals whose expertise aligns with your goals. This proactive approach can result in meaningful interactions that transcend virtual spaces, potentially leading to real-world collaborations.

Connecting with valuable mentors goes beyond simply finding someone willing to advise you—it requires a commitment to building a mutually beneficial relationship. Honest communication is key. Approach potential mentors with clarity about your objectives, and articulate how the relationship could be beneficial for both parties. Mentors are more likely to invest their time and resources if they perceive a reciprocal dynamic. Perhaps you bring fresh perspectives or unique skills to the table, or maybe your enthusiasm and drive are infectious. Emphasize these attributes to create a compelling case for collaboration.

As you navigate these avenues for establishing a mastermind alliance, remember that identifying potential mentors and collaborators is a deliberate process. Action steps include reaching out to people you admire, observing their work, and maintaining open lines of communication. Invite them to coffee, schedule introductory calls, or attend workshops they host. Demonstrating genuine interest in their experiences and insights sets the foundation for a strong professional relationship.

When considering your goals and the skills needed to achieve them, keep in mind that each connection is an opportunity to learn and grow. Be open to diverse perspectives and experiences, as they can provide new angles to solve challenges or innovate within your field. A well-rounded network not only supports individual success but also enriches the collective achievements of the alliance.

Action Steps for Building Your Mastermind Alliance

Establishing a mastermind alliance begins with clearly defining its purpose and goals. This foundational step ensures all members are aligned, promoting unity and focus within the group. When each individual understands the shared objective, they can contribute effectively, pooling their diverse skills and experiences for the alliance's benefit. For instance, consider a group of entrepreneurs aiming to scale their businesses. Their collective goal might be to share growth strategies, support each other in overcoming challenges, or inspire innovative ideas. By explicitly defining such purposes, the alliance sets a clear path to success.

Once goals are established, maintaining momentum is crucial, and regular meetings play a vital role in this. Whether conducted virtually or in-person, consistent gatherings facilitate ongoing communication and collaboration. These meetings serve as checkpoints, enabling members to update each other on progress, discuss obstacles, and brainstorm solutions collectively. The camaraderie and trust built through regular interactions enhance the group's cohesiveness. Imagine a scenario where tech pioneers meet weekly to exchange insights on industry trends. Regular interaction keeps them updated and fosters a continuous flow of fresh ideas and perspectives.

Moreover, setting ground rules and expectations is essential to creating a productive and respectful environment. Clear guidelines help manage discussions, ensuring everyone has an opportunity to speak and contribute. Rules could include time management protocols, confidentiality agreements, and decision-making processes. Such frameworks prevent misunderstandings and conflicts, promoting a culture of respect and professionalism. For instance, if one member monopolizes discussion time, predefined rules can guide a fair redistribution of speaking opportunities, maintaining balance and fairness within the group.

As the mastermind alliance evolves, continuous evaluation and adaptation become critical for long-term success. Over time, group dynamics may change due to factors like shifting member priorities or external market developments. Regular assessments can involve soliciting feedback from members, analyzing what works well and identifying areas for improvement. This adaptability ensures the alliance remains relevant and effective in achieving its objectives. An example could be a writing group that initially focuses on fiction but gradually incorporates non-fiction as member interests diversify. Adapting to these changes sustains engagement and productivity.

Bringing It All Together

In this chapter, we've explored the significant role that a supportive and knowledgeable team plays in achieving both personal and professional success. By being part of such a team, individuals can harness diverse perspectives, leading to innovative ideas and solutions. Whether it's through emotional support during challenging times or accessing a wealth of shared expertise, the benefits are clear. Teams foster resilience and create a sense of belonging among their members, driving progress and collective growth. We've also witnessed, through examples like Steve Jobs and Steve Wozniak, how different talents and strengths can merge to produce remarkable results.

Furthermore, this chapter has highlighted the importance of collaboration for sustained achievement. We discussed how being accountable to peers encourages goal attainment and enhances decision-making processes by considering multiple viewpoints. By identifying the right mentors and collaborators and building a mastermind alliance, individuals set themselves up for continuous learning and reflection. This environment not only propels personal development but also enriches the group as a whole. These insights serve as a guide for anyone aiming to build a strong network, emphasizing that true success often comes from building meaningful connections with others.

Chapter 8
Persistence Through Adversity

Persistence through adversity is essential for achieving success. This chapter delves into how enduring through setbacks and failures can lead to personal and professional growth. Adversity comes in various forms, affecting individuals across all facets of life. It doesn't matter if it presents itself as a challenging event, an unexpected change, or a setback in one's career; the impact on an individual's life can be profound. Examining adversity's nature reveals its universal presence and the need for developing resilience. This resilience becomes the cornerstone of overcoming obstacles, transforming stress into a learning experience, and eventually leading to success.

In this chapter, readers will explore how understanding the distinction between temporary setbacks and systemic challenges is crucial in navigating adversity effectively. By examining diverse examples, such as professional athletes who channel pressure into performance, the narrative highlights real-world applications of resilience. The chapter also presents insights from the lives of accomplished individuals, illustrating how their experiences in confronting significant obstacles have contributed to their eventual triumphs. Furthermore, the discussion extends to personal development, emphasizing how adversity helps clarify personal values and priorities. As readers progress through the chapter, they will gain practical knowledge and inspiration to harness their inner strength, turning adversity into opportunities for growth and fulfillment in their pursuits.

Understanding the Nature of Adversity

Adversity is a universal experience that each of us will face at different junctures in our lives. It does not discriminate between age, status, or ambitions —everyone encounters it in various forms. Whether it arrives as a personal challenge, professional setback, or an unexpected life event, adversity tests our limits and compels us to find strength within ourselves we may not have known existed. The inevitability of these obstacles makes understanding them crucial to personal and professional growth.

From a psychological perspective, adversity can significantly impact our mental state. On one hand, it presents stress and anxiety, imposing an emotional burden that can feel overwhelming. Yet, on the other hand, these experiences serve as the foundation for building resilience. Resilience, the capacity to recover quickly from difficulties, is often born out of repeated exposure to adversity. This transformative journey from stress to resilience is shaped by individual experiences and responses to challenges. For example, consider how sports athletes manage pressure; through repeated trials, they learn to channel stress into focused energy, ultimately enhancing their performance.

It's important to differentiate between temporary setbacks and systemic challenges. Temporary setbacks are those obstacles that appear suddenly but are often resolved with time and effort. An unexpected project failure or a missed opportunity might fall into this category. In contrast, systemic challenges are ingrained hurdles that persist over time and require strategic thinking and long-term solutions. Discrimination in the workplace or chronic economic hardship are examples of systemic challenges. Both categories demand unique responses tailored to their specific nature. While temporary setbacks might be navigated with quick problem-solving, systemic challenges often call for sustained advocacy and comprehensive strategies.

Understanding and overcoming adversity frequently lead to profound personal development and insight. Each challenge surmounted adds to a growing library of wisdom and experience, shaping one's character and fortifying future pursuits. For instance, entrepreneurs who navigate the failure of their startups often emerge with invaluable lessons about market demands and business strategy, positioning them for success in subsequent endeavors.

Moreover, the path through adversity often brings clarity to personal values and priorities. When faced with significant challenges, individuals are prompted to reassess what truly matters to them, leading to more aligned and fulfilling life choices. Consider someone who loses a job due to corporate downsizing; this adversity might open doors to exploring new career paths that align better with their passions and skills.

Furthermore, overcoming adversity encourages empathy and understanding toward others facing similar trials. The shared human experience of enduring difficulties fosters connection and community, as people draw on their own experiences to support and uplift others. This sense of community can provide additional strength and motivation when tackling personal challenges, creating a positive feedback loop of resilience and support.

Lessons from Oprah Winfrey's Journey

Oprah Winfrey's life story is a compelling testament to the power of persistence in overcoming adversity. Her journey from an impoverished and challenging childhood to becoming one of the world's most influential media moguls provides valuable insights for anyone aspiring to achieve personal and financial success despite significant obstacles.

Born into deep poverty in rural Mississippi, Oprah faced numerous hardships from an early age. Her mother, Vernita Lee, was a housemaid, and Oprah often lived with her grandmother on a farm where basic needs were scarce. This environment presented harsh realities that included inadequate access to resources and opportunities that many take for granted. The extent of these challenges didn't end there; she also encountered abuse during her childhood, which added emotional and psychological burdens to her already difficult circumstances. These experiences could have easily deterred her ambitions, yet they fueled her resolve to create a better future for herself.

Navigating these early trials required resilience and a belief in her own potential, something which Oprah cultivated over time. Education became a critical avenue for change. Despite her tumultuous home life, she excelled academically, earning a scholarship to Tennessee State University. This achievement marked a significant turning point, showcasing her ability to seize opportunities that aligned with her aspirations. It was during this phase that Oprah began to hone her skills in communication, a talent that would later define her career.

Her entry into television was another pivotal moment. Beginning as a news anchor before moving into talk shows, Oprah demonstrated an extraordinary capacity to connect with audiences through empathy and authenticity. At this juncture, the influence of mentors played a crucial role. People like Gayle King and Maya Angelou provided guidance and support, helping Oprah to navigate industry challenges and refine her unique style. These relationships were invaluable, offering insights and encouragement that inspired her to push boundaries and explore new possibilities within the media landscape.

The decisions Oprah made throughout her career illustrate not only strategic thinking but also a willingness to take risks. She chose to embrace unconventional approaches, such as creating content that focused on personal growth and empowerment rather than mere entertainment. This bold move resonated with viewers worldwide and set her apart from other media figures, cementing her status as a cultural icon. Her transition from television host to owning a multimedia empire exemplifies how embracing innovation can lead to unprecedented success.

Perhaps one of the most striking aspects of Oprah's journey is her unwavering tenacity. Even after achieving fame, she encountered periods of doubt and criticism. Instead of capitulating, Oprah continued to challenge herself, expanding into different ventures like publishing, acting, and philanthropy. Her commitment to lifelong learning and self-improvement underscores the theme of persistent pursuit of goals. By constantly evolving, Oprah has remained relevant and influential across generations, proving that adaptability is key to enduring success.

Oprah Winfrey's legacy extends beyond her professional accomplishments. As a philanthropist, she has made significant contributions to education and community development, impacting countless lives. Her dedication to giving back reflects the values that have guided her actions throughout her life—using her platform to inspire positive change and uplift those facing struggles akin to her own earlier experiences. Her ability to turn adversity into a catalyst for transformation serves as a powerful example for readers seeking motivation to overcome their own challenges.

In reflecting on Oprah's story, it becomes evident that her success was not merely a product of talent or opportunity but rather a result of persisting in the face of adversity. Her journey is characterized by a series of defining moments and intentional choices that led to continuous personal and professional growth. For ambitious individuals aiming to navigate their paths amid today's complexities, Oprah's experience offers both inspiration and practical lessons on harnessing inner strength to surmount setbacks.

Developing Resilience Through Journaling

In a world where setbacks and failures are inevitable, finding effective ways to process these experiences is crucial. Journaling emerges as a powerful tool in this journey, offering therapeutic benefits that can foster resilience. By putting pen to paper, individuals gain a safe space to explore their emotions, thoughts, and reactions. This act of writing becomes a release valve for pent-up emotions, allowing individuals to confront their challenges head-on. In recounting one's day, the victories, big or small, become more evident, shining amidst the adversities faced. This clarity not only helps manage stress but also boosts emotional intelligence, improving one's ability to navigate complex situations.

To maximize its benefits, adopting certain journaling techniques can significantly enhance personal growth. One popular method is the practice of gratitude lists. By regularly listing things one is thankful for, no matter how mundane, individuals begin to shift their focus from what went wrong to what is going right. This shift in perspective can cultivate positivity and optimism, essential traits for bouncing back from difficult times. Alongside gratitude lists, integrating reflective prompts into journaling can deepen self-awareness. Questions like "What did I learn today?" or "How can I handle similar situations differently?" encourage introspection, providing a framework to understand one's responses and strategies for improvement.

The interplay between journaling and mental health is well-supported by evidence. Research indicates that those who journal regularly often exhibit better mental health outcomes. These individuals tend to display decreased symptoms of anxiety and depression since they have honed their ability to process and articulate feelings. Additionally, the practice allows for a structured reflection, making it easier to identify patterns that might be contributing to stress or unhappiness. Over time, this improved mental health fosters increased adaptability, equipping individuals to adjust their approaches when faced with new challenges.

Journaling also plays a pivotal role in reframing perceived failures. Instead of viewing failures as endpoints, journaling encourages individuals to see them as stepping stones towards growth. By documenting the failure, its context, and the associated emotions, individuals gain distance from the immediate sting of disappointment. This separation offers the opportunity to reassess the situation objectively, identifying valuable lessons and alternative paths forward. Emphasizing lessons learned rather than mistakes made reshapes the narrative, transforming failures into catalysts for innovation and progress.

Developing resilience through journaling involves consistent practice and intentionality. A helpful guideline is to set aside a dedicated time each day for writing. Even if it's just ten minutes, this regularity builds a habit, weaving journaling into the fabric of daily life. It's also beneficial to create an environment conducive to reflection, perhaps by selecting a quiet corner or using a favorite notebook. When approaching journaling with an open mind, without self-imposed limitations or expectations, individuals allow themselves the freedom to explore thoughts unfiltered. This openness is key to uncovering deeper insights and cultivating resilience over time.

Moreover, overcoming adversity often requires a mindset shift, where failures are not seen as obstacles but as opportunities for growth. Journaling facilitates this shift by providing a tangible record of progress and learning. Revisiting old entries can be enlightening, showcasing how far one has come and reinforcing the belief that with persistence, similar future challenges can be tackled successfully. This practice reminds individuals of their capacity to endure hardship and emerge stronger, reinforcing a positive feedback loop of resilience-building.

While the personal nature of journaling allows for much flexibility, some structure can be advantageous. Utilizing a simple format like the three-part entry—where one writes about a challenge faced, the emotions experienced, and the lesson drawn—can provide consistency. This structure not only aids in processing emotions effectively but also ensures that the focus remains on growth and learning. Alternatively, incorporating visual elements, such as doodles or diagrams, can enrich the journaling process, especially for those who find words alone insufficient to convey their experiences fully.

Finally, embracing journaling as part of a broader strategy for personal development can yield significant dividends. As individuals become more adept at navigating adversity through written reflection, they often find it easier to address other areas of personal and professional life. The skills honed through journaling—such as emotional regulation, empathy, and critical thinking—are transferable, leading to enhanced interactions in work and social settings. Thus, journaling becomes not just a pastime but a foundational component of a resilient, adaptable life.

Reframing Failures as Lessons Learned

Persistence through adversity is a cornerstone of success, and shifting our perspective on failure plays a critical role in this journey. Instead of viewing failures as negative outcomes, we can transform them into valuable learning experiences. This change in mindset allows us to extract constructive feedback and grow from every setback.

Cognitive strategies provide a practical framework for this transformation. For instance, reframing one's thoughts about failure involves consciously altering how we react to missteps. When you encounter setbacks, instead of labeling them as failures, consider them experiments that offer insights into what didn't work. By analyzing the situation, identifying areas for improvement, and setting clear objectives for future attempts, individuals can use these experiences to finetune their approach. This process of reflection and adjustment not only aids in improving performance but also helps build resilience.

Real-world success stories further illustrate the potential of embracing initial failures. Thomas Edison famously failed thousands of times before inventing the light bulb. Each attempt was not a failure to him but rather a step towards mastering the invention. Similarly, J.K. Rowling faced numerous rejections from publishers before one finally agreed to publish "Harry Potter." These stories showcase how perseverance and a positive outlook on failures can lead to groundbreaking innovations and achievements. They remind us that success often lies just beyond the horizon of repeated efforts.

From a neurological standpoint, there is compelling evidence that embracing failure enhances creativity and problem-solving skills. The brain, when exposed to new challenges and allowed to make mistakes, forms new neural connections. This neuroplasticity is essential for creativity, enabling individuals to think outside the box and come up with innovative solutions. Studies have shown that allowing oneself to fail without fear encourages risk-taking and experimentation, both of which are crucial for developing creative thinking. Embracing failure thus becomes a method of training the brain to adapt and innovate continually.

Creating a mindset that views setbacks as stepping stones involves several actionable steps. First, cultivating self-awareness is key. Being mindful of your reactions to failure helps in recognizing patterns that may be holding you back. Practicing mindfulness techniques, like meditation or journaling, can assist in this endeavor by fostering a deeper understanding of one's thought processes.

Second, it's important to set realistic and flexible goals. Rather than pursuing rigid objectives, view each goal as a part of a larger learning curve. This approach reduces the fear of failure since each step, whether successful or not, contributes to overall progress. Additionally, adopting an attitude of curiosity can turn failures into opportunities for discovery. Ask yourself questions like, "What can I learn from this experience?" or "How can this inform my next move?"

Third, surrounding yourself with a supportive community can significantly impact your ability to bounce back from setbacks. Engaging with people who encourage growth and offer constructive criticism creates an environment conducive to learning. Furthermore, sharing experiences with others who have faced similar challenges can provide comfort and motivation, reinforcing the belief that failure is a universal aspect of growth.

Finally, practicing gratitude even in the face of failure can shift focus from what's lost to what's gained. Recognizing the lessons learned and the strength built through adversity helps maintain a positive outlook. Over time, this gratitude can transform into a sense of empowerment, fueling the drive to persevere despite obstacles.

In conclusion, changing our perspective on failure from negative to constructive is not merely about adopting a new mindset; it is about evolving our entire approach to challenges and setbacks. Through cognitive strategies, real-life examples, and neurological insights, we understand that failure is an essential component of the path to success. By developing a mindset that views setbacks as stepping stones, individuals can continuously learn, grow, and innovate, ultimately achieving their personal and professional goals. In this way, failure loses its sting and becomes a powerful catalyst for success.

Final Insights

In this chapter, we've explored how success often hinges on enduring through setbacks and failures. We've delved into the nature of adversity, recognizing that it is an inevitable part of life and a catalyst for growth. Through various perspectives, from psychological impacts to real-life examples like Oprah Winfrey's journey, we've seen how resilience is forged in the crucible of challenges. These stories highlight the importance of viewing failure not as an end but as an opportunity to learn and grow. The chapter encourages us to see adversity as a stepping stone toward achieving personal and professional success, illustrating that understanding and navigating setbacks can lead to profound development.

Furthermore, integrating practices like journaling and reframing failures as lessons learned offers practical strategies for building resilience. By documenting our experiences, we gain clarity and insight, enabling us to manage stress effectively and reframe difficulties as opportunities for growth. This approach fosters a shift in mindset—seeing failures as experiments rather than defeats—and encourages continuous learning. As we conclude this discussion, it's clear that persistence in the face of adversity is crucial for attaining long-term success. With these insights, ambitious individuals can harness inner strength and embrace challenges, ultimately transforming setbacks into powerful catalysts for progress.

Chapter 9
Overcoming Fear and Doubt

Overcoming fear and doubt is a journey that starts with understanding how these emotions serve as the greatest barriers to success. Fear, deeply embedded in human instincts, often stands as a formidable opponent, casting shadows on potential opportunities and clouding judgment when decisions must be made. While fear can sometimes sharpen focus, it frequently overwhelms, leading to uncertainty and hesitation. This chapter dives into dismantling such psychological barriers by exploring their fundamental causes and long-term impacts on personal and professional advancement.

In this exploration, the chapter examines the physiological roots of fear, detailing how mechanisms like the amygdala initiate responses that historically safeguarded human survival. However, in modern settings, this biological wiring can misalign with actual threats, hindering rational decision-making. By dissecting the chronic effects of fear on cognitive functions, the discussion unveils how persistent anxiety can erode memory and logical reasoning, creating cycles of self-perpetuating worry that sap potential. Through relatable scenarios and examples, readers are offered insights into the pervasive nature of fear's influence over choices and actions. Recognizing personal triggers forms the foundation for effective management strategies, and this chapter illuminates paths toward resilience. From identifying and categorizing fears to adopting mindfulness practices and incremental exposure techniques, the narrative guides readers in transforming fear into a catalyst for growth and empowerment, setting the stage for true achievement.

The Nature of Fear

Understanding the impact of fear on decision-making is crucial for anyone striving to achieve personal and professional success. Fear is one of the most potent emotional responses within human physiology, often influencing decisions beyond our awareness. To comprehend its full effect, we need to look at how it operates biologically and psychologically.

At the core of the fear response lies the amygdala, a small almond-shaped cluster of nuclei located in the brain's temporal lobe. When we perceive a threat, whether real or imagined, the amygdala is activated, setting off a chain reaction that prepares our bodies for fight-or-flight. This instinctual response can be traced back to our ancestors' need to survive imminent danger, but in modern contexts, it can significantly alter our decision-making processes.

For example, imagine you are preparing to pitch an innovative idea in a crucial business meeting. The mere thought of presenting might trigger your amygdala, leading to physiological changes like increased heart rate and heightened alertness. While these reactions can sharpen focus, they can also cloud judgment, prompting impulsive or overly cautious decisions. Recognizing this physiological underpinning provides insight into why some individuals experience paralyzing anxiety when faced with important choices.

Beyond the immediate response, chronic fear can have lasting effects on cognitive functions and rational thinking. Continuous exposure to stress-inducing situations without adequate coping mechanisms may impair memory, reduce concentration, and lower one's ability to process information logically. For instance, an entrepreneur constantly worried about the financial viability of their startup might display signs of tunnel vision, neglecting broader strategic opportunities due to an overwhelming sense of dread. In such cases, fear becomes self-perpetuating, as impaired decision-making leads to outcomes that reinforce the original fears.

If left unaddressed, fear can result in avoidance behaviors that further hinder progress. Avoidance, though often providing temporary relief from discomfort, can limit growth and opportunity. Consider a student with a fear of failure who consistently avoids challenging courses. This behavior, while reducing immediate stress, inadvertently curtails their academic potential and stifles personal development, leaving them less prepared for future challenges.

A critical step in overcoming fear involves recognizing its triggers and understanding its effects. This awareness forms the foundation for effective management strategies. Fear not only stems from external threats but is also influenced by past experiences, societal pressures, and personal insecurities. By identifying specific triggers, individuals can begin to dismantle the automatic fear response, replacing it with more constructive reactions.

Take, for example, someone with a fear of public speaking rooted in a childhood experience of embarrassment. By pinpointing this source, they can address the underlying fear through techniques such as cognitive restructuring or gradual exposure. Over time, this process diminishes the power of the original trigger, allowing for clearer, more confident decision-making.

Moreover, understanding fear's impact enables people to develop personalized strategies to mitigate its influence. Techniques such as mindfulness meditation, which encourages present-moment awareness, can help reduce the tendency to ruminate on worst-case scenarios. Similarly, practicing decision-making under low-stakes conditions can build resilience, making it easier to navigate high-pressure situations with composure.

Richard Branson's Case Study

Richard Branson stands as an icon of risk-taking, steering Virgin Group through uncharted waters to achieve monumental success. At the heart of his approach is a willingness to take calculated risks, a trait that has not only fueled Virgin's expansion but also serves as an inspiring blueprint for those seeking personal and financial advancement. Understanding this risk-taking mindset requires dissecting the strategic yet bold decisions that characterize Branson's entrepreneurial journey.

Branson's story exemplifies how calculated risks can transform vision into reality. When Branson launched Virgin Atlantic in 1984, he entered an industry dominated by established giants like British Airways. This decision was neither impulsive nor reckless; it was a calculated move based on thorough research and a keen understanding of market needs. He recognized a gap in customer service within the airline industry and bet on his ability to deliver a superior experience. This venture began with a single leased plane, but Branson's commitment to quality and innovation allowed Virgin Atlantic to carve out a significant market share over time. His ability to assess risks realistically while maintaining a clear focus on potential rewards highlights the importance of observation and calculation in risk-taking.

The mantra "screw it, let's do it," often associated with Branson, encapsulates the spirit necessary to seize opportunities when they arise. This attitude reflects not blind optimism but a readiness to act in the face of uncertainty. By embracing action over hesitation, individuals can unlock doors to possibilities they might otherwise miss. For instance, Branson's decision to expand into spaces such as music, mobile communications, and space tourism wasn't without challenges. Yet, this proactive stance propelled his ventures into diverse industries, demonstrating how acting on well-evaluated risks can lead to growth across multiple domains.

Failures are often perceived as stumbling blocks, but Branson views them as integral parts of the learning process. Rather than allowing setbacks to deter him, he uses these experiences to refine strategies and enhance resilience. One example is the short-lived Virgin Cola, which faced significant competition and ultimately failed to capture the market. Instead of seeing this as a defeat, Branson embraced it as a lesson in competitive dynamics, channeling insights gleaned from this failure into future projects. By reframing failures as valuable learning experiences, individuals can derive insights that prevent similar missteps, enabling continuous improvement and adaptation.

Persistence and resilience are crucial in navigating doubt and adversity, traits Branson embodies in his entrepreneurial pursuits. The path to success is rarely linear, and setbacks are inevitable. For Branson, the journey involves continually pushing boundaries and refusing to succumb to obstacles. His ventures thrive on adaptability and grit, qualities that play a pivotal role in overcoming doubt. This perseverance was evident when facing legal challenges and operational hurdles in various sectors. Through steadfast dedication and resourcefulness, Branson showcases the power of resilience in transforming doubt into assurance and progress.

To integrate Branson's lessons into one's own life, it's essential to cultivate a mindset that embraces risk and remains undeterred by failure. Evaluating risks with clear objectives and a comprehensive understanding of potential outcomes lays the groundwork for informed decision-making. Aspiring entrepreneurs and professionals must also foster a readiness to pivot when necessary, acknowledging that setbacks are opportunities for growth rather than permanent detours. Nurturing persistence ensures that temporary doubts do not hinder long-term goals, aligning efforts with Branson's philosophy of relentless pursuit.

Identifying Personal Fears

In the journey towards success, fear stands as a formidable barrier. To effectively overcome it, one must first recognize and categorize these fears, lending clarity and focus to personal growth efforts. Understanding the nature of each fear is crucial, which begins by differentiating between rational and irrational fears.

Rational fears are those grounded in reality, often based on potential threats or experiences that could cause harm or failure. These fears can be productive if they prompt necessary caution or preparation. For instance, a rational fear might involve financial instability when starting a new business, encouraging an entrepreneur to plan carefully. On the other hand, irrational fears usually arise from distorted perceptions or exaggerated scenarios. These are the ones that frequently lead to unnecessary anxiety and inaction, such as the fear of public speaking stemming from the unfounded belief that others will harshly judge every word. Recognizing this distinction helps not only in addressing fears but also in allocating energy and resources wisely.

Self-reflection is a powerful tool in uncovering subconscious fears that often lie beneath the surface, influencing behaviors and decisions without conscious awareness. Engaging in exercises such as journaling can provide insight into these hidden fears. Writing down daily thoughts and emotions may reveal patterns or triggers linked to deeper anxieties. Meditation or mindfulness practices can also facilitate this process, allowing individuals to observe their thoughts detachedly, identifying those subtle fears that might otherwise go unnoticed. By bringing subconscious fears to light, one gains the power to challenge and change them, leading to greater personal freedom and effectiveness.

Understanding the origin and impact of past experiences plays a significant role in dealing with current fears. Many fears stem from childhood or significant life events that left a lasting imprint. For example, someone who faced repeated criticism in school might continue to fear inadequacy in adult life, despite having evidence to the contrary. Evaluating these origins requires reviewing past experiences with an objective lens, discerning which memories contribute to ongoing fears. Therapy or counseling can aid in this exploration, offering professional insights and strategies for healing.

Once fears have been identified and understood, prioritization becomes key. Not all fears need immediate attention; focusing on those that most significantly impede progress toward goals is essential. This involves assessing the impact each fear has on your ambitions and determining where to direct efforts. A practical approach might include creating a list, ranking fears based on their influence on productivity or personal well-being. This method ensures that one's energy is concentrated on overcoming the most debilitating fears first, making gradual and meaningful advancements possible.

An effective guideline in tackling fears involves incremental steps towards confronting them. Begin by setting small, manageable goals designed to gradually expose yourself to the source of fear, reducing its power over time. Incremental progress fosters confidence, building a sense of accomplishment that motivates further action. While the ultimate goal is to conquer all fears, starting with the most impactful ensures that progress is both strategic and sustainable.

Taking Incremental Steps

To overcome fear and doubt, it's essential to adopt a strategy that involves gradual actions, thereby allowing us to face these emotions head-on. Starting with the establishment of small, achievable goals is an effective initial step. This approach breaks down the monumental task of overcoming fear into manageable parts, making it less intimidating and more approachable. For instance, if public speaking is a source of anxiety, consider setting a goal to speak up in a small group meeting. Achieving this small milestone can foster confidence and create momentum for tackling more significant challenges in the future.

Building on this foundation of small successes, we can incorporate the principles of exposure therapy to gradually diminish fear. Exposure therapy is widely recognized for its effectiveness in combating phobias and anxiety. By gradually increasing our exposure to the feared object or situation, we allow ourselves to adapt and grow more comfortable over time. Continuing with the public speaking example, after gaining comfort in smaller groups, one might progress to speaking at larger gatherings. The incremental exposure helps reduce fear as each experience builds upon the last, establishing a safer mental environment where fear loses its grip.

Alongside these individual efforts, seeking support systems or mentors plays a crucial role in this journey. Having someone who provides guidance and accountability can greatly enhance our ability to confront our fears. A mentor can offer invaluable insights based on their experiences, while support networks provide encouragement and reassurance. This communal element can be comforting, knowing there are others invested in your success. For instance, joining a speaking club like Toastmasters introduces you to a supportive community dedicated to improving communication skills, where feedback is constructive and growth is celebrated.

Equally important is the practice of positive visualization techniques. Visualization serves as a powerful tool to mentally rehearse overcoming obstacles before confronting them in reality. By vividly imagining ourselves successfully navigating daunting situations, we condition our minds to expect success rather than fear failure. Visualizing every detail—the sound of applause, the sense of accomplishment—strengthens our resolve and lessens anxiety. Athletes often use this method to prepare for competitions, so imagine yourself standing confidently on stage, delivering your speech with poise and clarity.

It's vital in our quest to overcome fear and doubt to remember that progress takes time and patience. Everyone's journey is unique, shaped by individual circumstances and challenges. However, by consistently setting small goals, applying gradual exposure, seeking mentorship, and visualizing successes, we're better equipped to dismantle the barriers erected by fear. Each step forward not only bolsters our courage but also transforms fear from a daunting obstacle into an opportunity for personal growth and empowerment.

The path to conquering fear is rarely linear; setbacks may occur, but they are part of the learning process. When we hit a roadblock, it is essential to reassess and recalibrate our efforts rather than viewing these moments as failures. These instances serve as reminders of the complexity of our emotions and the necessity to remain steadfast and adaptable. Progress should not be measured solely by grand achievements but by the subtle shifts in mindset—a growing willingness to take risks, an increase in self-assurance, or the diminishing power of previously paralyzing fears.

Ultimately, the transformation through fear isn't simply about eliminating all traces of worry. Instead, it is about altering our response to it, refining our relationship with fear such that it propels rather than paralyzes us. When fear and doubt are acknowledged without judgment and approached with deliberate action, they lose their supremacy. By embracing fear as a natural part of the human experience and using it as a catalyst for exploration and growth, we unlock potential within ourselves previously restrained by apprehension.

Incorporating these strategies into daily life doesn't require monumental changes overnight. It begins with small steps: jotting down simple goals, seeking out like-minded communities, or spending a few minutes each day immersed in visualization exercises. Over time, these practices cultivate a resilient mindset, ready to face whatever challenges lie ahead with optimism and determination. Before long, what once seemed insurmountable becomes just another stepping stone in the journey toward a more courageous, fulfilling life.

Transforming Fear into Motivation

Fear is often seen as a barrier, yet it can be channeled into a powerful driving force for personal development. This transformation begins with reframing fear into excitement. Imagine standing on the precipice of a daunting task—heart racing, palms clammy—and reinterpreting that anxiety as exhilarating anticipation. Research has shown that this cognitive shift can elevate your performance under pressure by harnessing the adrenaline rush that fear induces. Instead of perceiving fear as something to avoid, view it as an indicator of growth and potential success.

Mindfulness practices can further enhance your ability to stay calm and composed in the face of fear. Techniques such as meditation, deep breathing, and mindful awareness help anchor your thoughts in the present moment, reducing the overwhelming nature of anxiety. When you practice mindfulness regularly, you train your mind to observe fear without judgment or aversion. This cultivated presence creates a space between stimulus and response, allowing you to choose thoughtful actions over impulsive reactions. By remaining centered, you open up possibilities for creativity and innovative problem-solving, which can be particularly beneficial when navigating uncertainty.

In moments of fear, you can also tap into the energy it generates to fuel creativity and innovation. The heightened state of alertness prompted by fear primes the brain to search for novel solutions and strategies. Artists, writers, and entrepreneurs often talk about their best ideas emerging from periods of intense pressure and stress. Fear can propel you to think outside the box, encouraging risk-taking and experimentation. Consider Thomas Edison, who faced countless setbacks before successfully inventing the electric bulb; his persistent curiosity, driven by urgency and challenge, exemplifies leveraging fear to achieve remarkable outcomes.

To fully capitalize on fear's potential, adopting a growth mindset becomes essential. Coined by psychologist Carol Dweck, a growth mindset involves viewing failures and challenges as opportunities to learn rather than insurmountable obstacles. When you embrace this perspective, fear loses its power to paralyze because you begin to see each setback as a stepping stone toward mastery and personal improvement. By fostering resilience and adaptability, a growth mindset equips you to confront fears with a proactive attitude, transforming intimidating situations into platforms for development.

Let's delve into how these approaches interact in real-world scenarios. Picture a professional preparing for an important presentation. Initially, the prospect might trigger intense fear, freezing thoughts and heightening nerves. However, by reframing this fear as excitement, the individual acknowledges the opportunity inherent in the situation—a chance to showcase expertise and make an impact. Through mindful breathing, they ground themselves, alleviating tension and securing mental clarity. As preparation continues, the fear-induced adrenaline sharpens focus, prompting creative ways to engage the audience. With a growth mindset, the presenter views any mishaps not as failures but as valuable learning experiences for future improvements.

Guidelines can solidify these concepts into actionable steps. Start by embracing challenges that naturally elicit fear, consciously interpreting them as adventures rather than threats. Incorporate a daily mindfulness routine to build mental resilience. When fear arises, identify its source, acknowledge its presence, and redirect the accompanying energy toward constructive endeavors. Cultivate a habit of reflection, pondering what each experience teaches you and how it contributes to your personal evolution.

Moreover, it's crucial to share stories of individuals who have effectively harnessed fear for personal growth. Steve Jobs, co-founder of Apple, often spoke about his fear of failure motivating him to break boundaries and innovate continually. His relentless pursuit of excellence in the face of fear led to groundbreaking technological advancements that reshaped industries. Likewise, athletes frequently utilize pre-competition jitters to sharpen their competitive edge, demonstrating the universal application of transforming fear into progress across various fields.

Bringing It All Together

In this chapter, we explored how fear can act as a significant barrier to success, influencing decision-making and shaping our responses to challenges. We delved into the biological roots of fear, illustrating how the amygdala triggers fight-or-flight reactions that, while useful for survival, can impair rational thinking in modern contexts. By examining case studies such as Richard Branson's risk-taking journeys, we've seen how an understanding of fear's effects can lead to transformative strategies that turn perceived limitations into motivators for growth. Recognizing the triggers of fear and employing techniques like cognitive restructuring or gradual exposure helps individuals dismantle automatic fear responses, fostering clearer decision-making.

As we conclude, it's important to embrace the potential within fear, transforming it from an obstacle into a source of motivation. Techniques such as mindfulness and positive visualization allow us to remain grounded and focused, reducing fear's grip on our actions. Embracing a growth mindset further enables us to view challenges and setbacks as opportunities for learning and improvement rather than insurmountable barriers. With these strategies, fear becomes less about avoidance and more about exploration, guiding ambitious individuals toward personal and professional advancement. This approach empowers readers to harness fear constructively, paving their unique path to success with resilience and adaptability.

Chapter 10
The Subconscious Mind and Success

The subconscious mind is a powerful force that quietly influences our daily actions and decisions. Its impact on success is profound, yet often overlooked by those who focus primarily on conscious strategies for achievement. Operating beneath the level of awareness, the subconscious mind processes and stores countless experiences, shaping our beliefs and behaviors in ways we might not fully comprehend. When tapped into thoughtfully, the subconscious can become a reliable ally in the pursuit of personal and professional success, guiding us toward paths aligned with our deepest aspirations and goals.

In this chapter, we delve into the various techniques that can help harness the power of the subconscious mind to achieve success. Readers will explore how mental programming through positive affirmations can reshape limiting beliefs into empowering ones, paving the way for enhanced self-belief and confidence. The chapter also uncovers the significance of visualization as a tool for aligning subconscious thoughts with conscious objectives, offering a glimpse into how vividly imagining desired outcomes can translate these visions into reality. Furthermore, the discussion extends to integrating such practices seamlessly into daily routines, illustrating how consistent application can create long-lasting patterns conducive to success. By embracing these methods, individuals can unlock the potential within themselves, transforming their internal narratives and aligning their actions with their ultimate ambitions.

Programming Your Mind for Achievement

Unlocking the potential of the subconscious mind is a profound and often underappreciated journey towards achieving success. The subconscious mind, an ever-active powerhouse beneath our awareness, governs many of our daily habits and beliefs. These subconscious patterns influence actions and decisions without direct conscious control, shaping how we navigate life's opportunities and challenges. By understanding this vast reservoir of thoughts and emotions, individuals can harness its power to pave a path toward personal and professional success.

To truly grasp the impact of programming the subconscious for success, it's essential to recognize its role as a foundation for our behaviors. Much like an iceberg, what lies beneath the surface—the subconscious—far exceeds what is visible or consciously acknowledged. It stores ingrained responses and automatic behaviors that are often the result of past conditioning or habitual thinking. As such, tapping into this part of the mind demands deliberate effort and conscious intent to cultivate beneficial patterns over unwanted or limiting ones.

One effective method to begin rewiring the subconscious mind involves using positive affirmations. These are deliberate statements that reinforce desired beliefs and attitudes. By regularly engaging in affirmations, individuals can gradually foster new beliefs about themselves and their capabilities. This acts like planting seeds of confidence and self-belief, allowing these traits to flourish over time. For instance, repeating phrases like "I am capable of achieving my goals" or "I am deserving of success" eventually ingrains these ideas so deeply that they become integral parts of one's self-concept and daily behavior.

Visualization techniques further complement affirmations by adding a multidimensional aspect to mental programming. Visualization involves vividly imagining specific outcomes or scenarios related to one's goals. When practiced consistently, it serves as a mental rehearsal, enabling individuals to experience success in their minds before it manifests in reality. Visualizing oneself successfully closing a business deal, acing an exam, or confidently delivering a presentation cultivates familiarity with those moments, transforming nervous anticipation into confident execution when faced in the real world.

The beauty of combining affirmations and visualization lies in their ability to align the subconscious mind with the conscious pursuit of goals. Such alignment enhances motivation and persistence, vital components for overcoming obstacles and maintaining focus over extended periods. By establishing a clear link between subconscious patterns and desired outcomes, individuals can create a seamless integration between dreams and tangible achievements. The resulting harmony empowers them to remain steadfast in their endeavors, even when confronted with setbacks or challenges.

Consistent mental programming extends beyond mere repetition; it involves embedding these practices into daily routines and making them second nature. This requires dedication but pays off significantly by fostering an unyielding drive towards one's aspirations. The brain, responsive to repeated inputs, gradually alters its neural pathways to support these intentions. Autopilot behaviors and default thought patterns begin aligning with what has been methodically cultivated through focused efforts. Consequently, pursuing goals no longer feels forced or strained, as the mind automatically gravitates towards actions conducive to success.

Neurological research supports the transformative impact of repeated thoughts and images on the brain's structure and function. Studies indicate that our brains possess remarkable plasticity, meaning they can reorganize and adapt based on experiences and mental input. This neuroplasticity suggests that by intentionally filling our minds with positive and goal-oriented content, we can physically reshape our brains to favor success-oriented behaviors. With every mental rehearsal or affirmation recited, we slowly carve new pathways that facilitate easier access to creativity, insight, and determination.

Incorporating these practices does not require elaborate rituals or extensive time commitments. A few minutes each day dedicated to affirmations and visualization can set powerful changes in motion. Perhaps starting the day with a brief session of envisioning one's most important objectives and mentally rehearsing the steps to achieve them could establish a proactive mindset. Similarly, ending each day with reflection on progress made and affirmations of continued belief reinforces resilience and optimism for the future.

Ultimately, the relationship between the subconscious mind and success underscores the significance of intentional mental conditioning. By embracing tools like affirmations and visualization, individuals can harness the innate power of their subconscious to steer their lives towards environments ripe with achievement and satisfaction. Through unwavering commitment and mindful attention to mental programming, they transform from passive observers of their destinies to active architects, consciously crafting paths aligned with their deepest ambitions.

Case Study: Kobe Bryant's Visualization Techniques

Kobe Bryant's remarkable career in basketball serves as a testament to the power of mental focus strategies. Among these practices, vivid visualization stood out as one of his primary techniques. Before stepping onto the court, Bryant would mentally rehearse various scenarios, imagining himself executing plays with precision and finesse. This practice was more than mere daydreaming; it was an intensive mental rehearsal where he visualized every movement, from dribbles and passes to accurate shots at the basket. By doing so, he not only built a sense of familiarity and comfort but also boosted his confidence significantly, allowing him to perform under pressure with remarkable poise.

Visualization was just one aspect of Bryant's extensive mental preparation. He went further by anticipating potential challenges that could arise during a game. Whether it was dealing with a particularly formidable opponent or navigating unfavorable match conditions, Bryant prepared his mind for these possibilities by strategizing solutions ahead of time. This foresight enabled him to maintain a high level of adaptability on the court.

When an unexpected situation arose, Bryant had already envisioned a way to handle it, allowing him to make quick decisions and effective adjustments without being rattled by stress or anxiety.

Kobe Bryant's dedication to mental training was evident throughout his career. His rigorous approach wasn't limited to physical workouts and skill development; he placed equal importance on cultivating a strong mental attitude. This commitment is widely believed to have been a crucial factor in his ability to consistently deliver high-level performances. Bryant's resilience in the face of setbacks and his unwavering drive towards excellence were deeply rooted in his mental preparedness. It's this mental fortitude that allowed him to bounce back from defeats and injuries, often emerging stronger and more determined than before.

The effectiveness of Bryant's mental strategies did not go unnoticed by experts in the field of sports psychology. Professionals widely advocate for similar techniques, underscoring their role in enhancing an athlete's focus and reducing performance-related anxiety. Visualization, for instance, has been shown to engage the brain in ways that are similar to physical practice, reinforcing neural pathways associated with specific skills and actions. As athletes visualize themselves succeeding, their brains register these imagined achievements almost as vividly as real ones, creating a positive feedback loop that enhances both confidence and performance.

Moreover, embracing mental focus strategies can lead to significant improvements beyond the realm of sports. Professionals across various fields can apply these techniques to sharpen their focus, manage stress, and improve overall performance in challenging situations. Like Kobe Bryant, individuals seeking personal and professional advancement can benefit from visualizing desired outcomes and preparing mentally for obstacles they may encounter along the way. This proactive approach to mental readiness empowers people to tackle challenges head-on, equipped with a strategic mindset geared toward success.

While physical prowess and technical skill are vital, Bryant's legacy highlights the equally crucial role of mental conditioning in achieving greatness. His story offers valuable lessons for anyone aiming to excel in their endeavors, encouraging them to harness the untapped power of their subconscious minds. Through practiced visualization and meticulous mental preparation, Kobe Bryant created a blueprint for success that transcends the boundaries of basketball and resonates with aspiring individuals worldwide.

Action Steps: Cultivating a Meditation Practice

Establishing a meditation routine is a powerful way to tap into the potential of the subconscious mind and achieve success. Meditation, in its essence, is a practice that encourages stillness and reflection. This stillness allows individuals to connect with their deeper thoughts, making it an ideal tool for reducing stress and promoting mental clarity. In our fast-paced world, stress is often an unavoidable part of life, yet it can cloud judgment and hinder effective decision-making. By cultivating a habit of regular meditation, individuals can mitigate stress levels, leading to sharper thinking and improved problem-solving abilities.

Mindfulness meditation, specifically, has been shown to enhance attention control and emotional regulation. It promotes an awareness of the present moment, allowing practitioners to observe their thoughts without judgment. This heightened state of awareness aids in focusing on goals with a clear and undistracted mind. When one can control their attention effectively, distractions become less intrusive, and maintaining focus on long-term objectives becomes second nature. Furthermore, emotional regulation, which is strengthened through mindfulness practices, equips individuals to manage emotions constructively, reducing impulsive reactions and fostering a steady pursuit of success.

Incorporating guided visualizations within meditation sessions can further amplify these benefits. Visualizations involve forming vivid mental images of desired outcomes or states of being. This technique can reinforce positive mental states and aspirations, effectively programming the subconscious mind towards achieving specific goals. For instance, an entrepreneur might visualize successfully launching a new product, experiencing the satisfaction and confidence accompanying this achievement. Such imagery serves as a rehearsal, preparing the mind to recognize and pursue opportunities aligned with these visualized experiences.

Scientific studies have provided compelling evidence supporting the transformative effects of meditation on brain structure. Research indicates that consistent meditation can lead to changes in brain areas associated with concentration and learning capacity. The prefrontal cortex, responsible for decision-making and cognitive behavior, shows increased thickness following regular meditation practice. This structural change contributes to enhanced cognitive functions, allowing individuals to approach challenges with greater ingenuity and resilience. Additionally, the amygdala, a region linked to emotional responses, tends to shrink with consistent meditation, leading to a calmer, more balanced emotional state.

Developing a daily meditation routine doesn't require extensive time commitments but rather a dedication to practice. Starting with as little as five to ten minutes a day can create significant shifts in mindset and perception. As individuals grow accustomed to the practice, extending meditation sessions can deepen its benefits. Conveniently, meditation can be practiced almost anywhere—whether at home, in the workplace, or even during a quiet moment in nature. This accessibility makes it an adaptable tool for anyone seeking personal and professional growth.

For newcomers to meditation, various apps and online resources offer guided sessions tailored to different needs, from stress relief to enhancing creativity. These tools can provide structure and motivation, especially during the initial stages of building a routine. Over time, individuals may choose to personalize their practice, incorporating elements such as deep breathing techniques, body scans, or mantra repetitions to suit their unique preferences and goals.

An unexpected advantage of meditation is its ability to improve interpersonal relationships. By fostering empathy and understanding through increased self-awareness, individuals often find themselves communicating more effectively and compassionately with others. This enhanced social interaction can lead to better networking and collaboration, essential components of success in any field.

Meditation is not a one-size-fits-all solution; different approaches resonate with different individuals. Some may find peace in silent meditation, while others thrive with the guidance of audio prompts. Exploring various techniques can help identify the most effective method for personal development. Moreover, as life circumstances evolve, adapting one's meditation practice to meet new challenges and aspirations is crucial for sustained growth.

The journey into meditation is deeply personal, but sharing experiences with peers or joining meditation groups can provide additional support and encouragement. Engaging with a community can foster accountability, helping individuals maintain consistency in their practice. Additionally, exchanging insights can reveal new perspectives and deepen understanding, enriching the overall meditation experience.

Creating a Mindful Environment

Creating an environment that encourages mental programming and productivity begins with addressing the physical space around us. A clutter-free, organized environment can significantly enhance focus and efficiency. Disorganization often leads to distraction, pulling attention away from tasks and diminishing mental clarity. On the other hand, a tidy workspace removes visual interruptions, allowing the mind to concentrate on the task at hand. For instance, consider the difference between working in an office where papers are strewn about versus one where everything is neatly arranged. The latter not only reduces stress but also boosts productivity by creating a sense of order.

In addition to organization, incorporating elements that promote relaxation and creativity can further enrich your environment. Calming colors like blues and greens have been shown to reduce stress, while natural elements like plants can improve air quality and mental wellbeing. Scents also play a crucial role in influencing mood and cognition. Lavender, for example, is known for its calming effects, potentially lowering anxiety and promoting a peaceful working atmosphere. By designing a space that integrates these soothing aspects, you create a haven for creative thought and efficient work processes.

Digital mindfulness is another essential aspect of fostering a productive environment in our technology-driven world. It's easy to fall into the trap of incessant notifications and digital distractions, which can lead to overstimulation and a lack of mental clarity. To counter this, deliberate management of technology use is necessary. This involves setting boundaries for device usage, such as designated screen-free times or using apps that limit social media consumption. These practices help maintain focus and allow the mind to rest, ultimately improving overall productivity.

Furthermore, establishing routines and rituals can condition the mind for productive states. Routines, whether it's starting the day with a set morning routine or taking regular breaks, help reduce decision fatigue and streamline work processes. Consistency through rituals also provides structure, minimizing the energy spent on transitioning between tasks or deciding what to tackle next. For example, beginning each workday with a brief period of meditation or goal-setting can mentally prepare you for the tasks ahead, reducing friction and enhancing productivity.

Action Steps: Create a meditation or mindfulness practice. Incorporating these practices into daily routines can be transformative. Meditation doesn't require extensive time commitments; even five to ten minutes a day can yield significant benefits. Regular meditation allows the subconscious mind to unwind and reset, aiding in stress reduction and mental clarity. By consciously integrating such practices, you pave the way for more focused and effective work habits, aligning the mind towards achieving success.

Adopting a Growth Mindset

In the journey towards personal and financial success, harnessing the power of a growth mindset can be transformative. This mindset, rooted in the belief that abilities and intelligence can be developed through dedication and hard work, becomes an essential tool for continual improvement and resilience.

When individuals view challenges as opportunities for learning rather than obstacles, they open themselves up to a path of perseverance and innovation. Rather than avoiding tasks out of fear of failure, embracing difficulties as stepping stones allows one to experiment with new ideas and learn from each attempt, whether successful or not. For instance, Thomas Edison famously faced countless setbacks before inventing the light bulb, yet he perceived each failed attempt as valuable feedback rather than defeat. This perspective shifts the focus from immediate success to long-term growth, fostering a mindset where setbacks are seen as integral components of the learning process.

Effort plays a pivotal role in this developmental journey. Recognizing effort as the pathway to mastery mitigates the fear of failure and reinforces dedication. When effort is genuinely appreciated, it encourages a culture of persistence. Taking on new tasks or skill development often involves trial and error; however, those who understand that effort is the unifying force behind achievement find joy in the process itself. Consider the story of J.K. Rowling, whose manuscript for Harry Potter was rejected multiple times. Her dedication to refining her work, acknowledging each rejection as part of her effort-driven path, underscores the profound impact of tenacity.

Curiosity and openness to feedback serve as catalysts for personal and professional development. Those willing to ask questions and actively seek constructive criticism position themselves advantageously for adaptation and growth. Curiosity drives exploration into new realms of knowledge and understanding, while feedback provides critical insights that might not be apparent otherwise. In entrepreneurial contexts, many businesses thrive by soliciting customer feedback to improve products, demonstrating how curiosity and receptivity contribute directly to success.

Psychological research supports the notion that cultivating a growth mindset laids the groundwork for greater achievement across various domains. Studies indicate that individuals who believe in their capacity to grow tend to embrace change more readily and show better performance across diverse fields. This adaptability, a cornerstone of the growth mindset, enables people to navigate through evolving landscapes—whether in technology, business, education, or personal endeavors—by continually updating skills and perspectives to meet new demands.

Adopting a growth mindset requires concerted efforts in shifting perspectives and behaviors. It involves recognizing that talent and intelligence are not fixed traits but rather aspects that can blossom with time and practice. By integrating this mindset into daily life, one begins to foster resilience—a necessary trait for enduring life's inevitable ups and downs. The stories of renowned figures who embraced growth-centric attitudes underscore its importance. They illuminate that failure does not mark an endpoint but rather signifies another opportunity to refine and try again.

For ambitious individuals seeking success, the concept of a growth mindset offers hope and practical strategies. It invites them to tackle challenges head-on, value sustained effort, welcome constructive feedback, and stay adaptable in the face of uncertainty. This approach not only enhances personal satisfaction but also sets the stage for breakthroughs.

Ultimately, the benefits derived from a growth mindset extend beyond individual success to influence communities and organizations. When leaders cultivate environments that encourage continuous learning and reward persistence, they inspire teams to strive collectively towards shared goals. Through shared growth experiences, these teams become more cohesive and innovative, driving overall success.

Final Insights

In this chapter, we've explored the profound impact of harnessing the subconscious mind for success. By delving into the power held within our subconscious, we can understand how it subtly influences our actions and choices, shaping our paths toward achievement. Techniques such as positive affirmations and visualization were highlighted as effective tools to reprogram these deep-seated patterns. These methods enable us to plant seeds of confidence and self-belief, allowing them to blossom into tangible results. The examples provided, including those from notable figures like Kobe Bryant, illuminate the real-world benefits of aligning subconscious intentions with conscious efforts. Through diligent practice, individuals can create a harmonious connection between their deepest ambitions and everyday actions.

As we continue on this journey towards personal and professional success, embedding these mental strategies into daily routines becomes essential. Consistent application of affirmations and visualization enriches our mindset, paving the way for long-term perseverance and resilience. This chapter emphasizes that nurturing a proactive relationship with our subconscious mind transforms us from passive observers into active architects of our destiny. By doing so, we are better equipped to navigate life's challenges, turning setbacks into growth opportunities and ensuring that our aspirations align seamlessly with achievable goals.

Chapter 11
Beyond Wealth: Redefining Success

Redefining success is an essential undertaking in a world where traditional benchmarks often revolve around wealth and material achievements. To truly understand what it means to be successful, it's imperative to look beyond financial gains and delve into elements that provide deeper fulfillment and a lasting legacy. This chapter invites readers to explore the various dimensions of success which extend far beyond monetary wealth, incorporating aspects such as purpose, relationships, and impact. By shifting focus from external validations to internal satisfaction, one can aspire to lead a more enriched and balanced life. It is not merely about reaching financial pinnacles but about nurturing the core components that contribute to overall happiness and societal contribution.

As you journey through this chapter, you will encounter insightful discussions on how purpose acts as the compass guiding individuals towards meaningful achievements. The narrative unfolds to illustrate how aligning core values with one's actions transforms ordinary pursuits into fulfilling missions. Moreover, the chapter examines the role of relationships in broadening our understanding of success. You'll discover how personal and professional bonds enrich our lives, providing support and fostering resilience during challenging times. Finally, the chapter delves into the concept of impact as a critical measure of success, exploring how contributions to society and the environment leave enduring marks and create a legacy that transcends generations. Through examples and reflections, readers are encouraged to redefine their personal definitions of success by weaving together purpose, relationships, and impactful actions, ultimately crafting a holistic and meaningful life narrative.

Purpose as a Core Component of Success

Purpose is the compass that provides direction and motivation, guiding individuals through both their personal and professional journeys. Imagine navigating a vast ocean without a map or a clear destination; that's what life can feel like without a defined purpose. This central sense of purpose not only fuels determination but also acts as an anchor, offering stability during turbulent times. When challenges arise, those with a strong purpose are often better equipped to push forward, drawing strength from their clear understanding of why they are on their chosen path. Purpose infuses daily routines with meaning, transforming ordinary tasks into fulfilling missions.

The alignment of daily activities with one's values and long-term goals is where personal fulfillment truly comes alive. Consider an entrepreneur whose core value is innovation, who dreams of reshaping industries. Every step in their career, from attending seminars to networking with like-minded innovators, becomes an expression of this value, contributing to a greater sense of satisfaction and achievement. This congruence between daily actions and overarching ambitions ensures that their life's work isn't just about personal gain but is deeply rooted in genuine passion and intention. Fulfillment arises when our internal motivations harmonize with external endeavors, creating a cohesive narrative of success.

A well-defined purpose also sharpens decision-making, serving as a guiding principle when faced with crossroads. In a world brimming with choices, having a clear purpose helps individuals prioritize options that align with their ultimate aspirations. For instance, professionals mindful of ethical considerations might decline lucrative offers that conflict with their commitment to sustainability. By doing so, they forge paths consistent with their purpose, ensuring decisions reflect their authentic selves. This clarity not only minimizes regret but also strengthens confidence, knowing each choice is aligned with a larger vision. Purpose acts as a sieve, filtering out distractions and honing focus on what truly matters.

Moreover, research highlights the link between a strong sense of purpose and improved health outcomes. Individuals grounded in purpose often experience lower stress levels, reduced risk of chronic diseases, and increased longevity. There is a profound connection between the mind's sense of fulfillment and the body's physical health. People with purpose-driven lives tend to adopt healthier lifestyles, engage in meaningful social relationships, and maintain active mental and emotional states. These factors collectively contribute to improved well-being, illustrating how deeply interconnected purpose and health truly are.

The Role of Relationships in Achieving Success

In today's fast-paced world, the notion of success is rapidly evolving. While financial prosperity is often seen as a benchmark, it's important to look beyond wealth in our journey toward true success. Relationships play a pivotal role in this broader definition, acting as a cornerstone upon which various facets of life are built.

Strong relationships are vital for providing emotional support and resilience, especially during challenging times. Consider the comforting presence of family members or close friends who stand by you during life's ups and downs. When faced with obstacles, having someone to rely on can lessen the burden and provide encouragement. This network of support not only strengthens your resolve but also enhances your ability to bounce back from setbacks. The assurance that comes from knowing you're not alone fosters a sense of confidence, allowing you to face challenges head-on.

Additionally, relationships extend beyond personal circles into professional realms, where building networks is crucial for career advancement and opportunities. In today's interconnected world, who you know can significantly impact what doors open for you. A strong professional network can lead to job prospects, partnerships, or mentorship opportunities that might not have been accessible otherwise. Networking events, conferences, and social platforms offer avenues to connect with others in your field, fostering mutually beneficial relationships. These connections can be invaluable, providing insights and guidance that propel your career forward.

Moreover, meaningful connections contribute significantly to one's mental well-being and happiness. Humans are inherently social creatures, and genuine interactions are essential for emotional health. Engaging in conversations, sharing experiences, and simply having a laugh with someone you care about enriches life in indescribable ways. Studies repeatedly show that individuals with strong personal ties often enjoy better mental health, increased happiness levels, and even longer lifespans. The simple act of being understood and valued by another person can create a profound sense of belonging and contentment.

Another dimension to explore is how collaborations and partnerships enhance innovation and problem-solving capabilities. When people come together, they bring diverse perspectives and skills to the table, creating fertile ground for creativity and innovation. Collaborating allows problems to be addressed through multiple viewpoints, leading to solutions that might not have emerged in isolation. Think of the most successful companies; they thrive on teamwork, pooling talents and ideas to drive progress. This synergy often results in breakthroughs that advance industries and pave new paths forward.

To harness the full potential of relationships in achieving success, it's essential to approach them with intention and authenticity. Making genuine efforts to connect with others, listening actively, and expressing appreciation builds the trust that forms the foundation of enduring relationships. In both personal and professional contexts, these actions help cement bonds that are resilient to time and distance.

Furthermore, cultivating relationships requires effort and consistency. Much like tending to a garden, regular interaction and nurturing are necessary for relationships to flourish. This could mean scheduling regular catch-ups with friends, staying connected with colleagues, or simply reaching out to check in. By investing time and energy into these connections, you create a robust support system that can be leaned on during different stages of your journey.

While it may seem daunting to manage numerous relationships in today's busy world, the rewards far outweigh the challenges. Prioritizing quality over quantity ensures that your interactions are meaningful and truly supportive. Knowing which relationships to invest in and how to maintain them is a skill that can greatly enhance one's success and overall life satisfaction.

Impact as a Measure of Success

In today's world, success is often synonymous with the amount of wealth accrued or the tangible achievements one can display. Yet, redefining success means looking beyond these traditional metrics and focusing on the impact one has on society and the environment. Impactful contributions not only create a lasting legacy but also transcend generations, leaving a mark long after personal or corporate accolades have faded.

For instance, initiatives that aim to improve societal welfare or preserve the environment serve as enduring legacies. Consider community-driven projects that build sustainable local economies or environmental programs that restore natural landscapes—these actions resonate deeply within communities and inspire future generations to continue the work. Such endeavors shift the focus from individual gain to collective progress, fortifying the notion that success entails making positive changes that endure over time.

Measuring success by impact encourages individuals and organizations to adopt sustainable and ethical practices. By prioritizing how actions affect both people and the planet, decision-makers are more likely to implement strategies that promote long-term health and well-being. For example, companies focused on reducing their carbon footprint or supporting fair trade stand out as pioneers in ethical business practice. Their commitment to positive change not only demonstrates responsible leadership but also sets off a chain reaction that encourages others to follow suit, thereby embedding sustainability deep into the core fabric of their operations.

Moreover, individuals and organizations that make significant impacts often enjoy increased trust and a stellar reputation. Trust, much like respect, is earned through consistent actions that demonstrate reliability and integrity. When companies prioritize impact, they build a reservoir of goodwill among consumers, employees, and stakeholders. This trust becomes a valuable asset, enhancing brand loyalty and creating robust, resilient relationships that withstand the test of time. Similarly, individuals who dedicate themselves to causes greater than their personal ambitions are celebrated and remembered for their service, fueling inspiration and aspiration in others around them.

Impactful actions have the power to inspire others and drive collective progress towards common goals. Acts of kindness, innovation for social good, and environmental stewardship capture the imagination and hearts of many. These stories of impact ripple through societies, inspiring individuals to contribute in ways that align with their capabilities and passions. The compounding effect of such inspiration energizes communities, fostering an environment where creativity and compassion flourish hand in hand.

In shaping our understanding of success through the lens of impact, we open doors for new narratives that highlight the importance of collaboration and purpose. While traditional measures of success may emphasize individual achievement, impact-based success reinforces the idea that we're all part of a larger ecosystem. Our actions, no matter how small, can influence greater outcomes that benefit everyone.

As individuals and organizations redefine what it means to be successful, integrating impact into the core of one's goals becomes paramount. It calls for a reassessment of priorities, where the emphasis is placed not just on achieving milestones but on the quality and sustainability of those achievements. By doing so, we align success with values that uphold human dignity and environmental preservation, steering us towards a future where the true worth of success lies in the positive differences made within our shared world.

Case Study: Melinda French Gates' Philanthropic Mission

Melinda French Gates has long been a prominent figure when discussing philanthropy, but what sets her apart is her distinctive approach to redefining wealth. Wealth, traditionally perceived as an accumulation of financial assets, finds a refreshing transformation through her philanthropic efforts. Gates, leveraging her significant resources, focuses on initiatives that tackle pressing issues in global health and education. Her efforts illuminate how wealth can be a powerful tool for societal change rather than just personal gain.

A pivotal part of this redefinition lies in how Melinda French Gates addresses global health challenges. The impact of her contributions through the Bill & Melinda Gates Foundation is immense. By directing funds towards combating diseases like malaria and tuberculosis, she expands the understanding of wealth by channeling it into life-saving ventures. Gates's dedication is evident in initiatives such as vaccination programs aimed at reducing child mortality rates in developing countries. These efforts convey a message: true success encompasses enhancing the well-being of society and not merely accumulating riches.

In parallel, her investment in education further underscores this redefined notion of wealth. Through various projects, Gates endeavors to provide equal educational opportunities. Initiatives focusing on increasing access to quality education in underserved regions reveal an underlying belief that wealth should bring empowerment. By fostering environments where learning thrives, her philanthropy transforms lives and communities, highlighting the capacity of wealth to bridge educational gaps and create a foundation for a brighter future.

Furthermore, her focus on gender equality makes a compelling case for the transformative power of targeted philanthropic efforts. Melinda French Gates has exhibited unwavering commitment to empowering women around the globe. Her Pivotal Ventures initiative exemplifies this, as it invests in innovative solutions to advance gender equity. By advocating for women's rights and opportunities, she challenges traditional paradigms of wealth, illustrating how investments in gender equality can lead to broader societal transformations. In her view, championing women's causes is not only about fairness but also about unlocking vast potentials within societies.

Another dimension of Gates's philanthropic model is her collaborative approach, which significantly amplifies the reach and effectiveness of her contributions. Collaboration transcends individual capability; it creates synergies that maximize impact. Gates frequently partners with governments, other nonprofit organizations, and the private sector to forge alliances that drive meaningful outcomes. Her work with international partners showcases how aligning missions and pooling resources leads to greater efficacy. This cooperative framework does more than achieve immediate goals; it sets the stage for sustained progress by involving diverse stakeholders in collective problem-solving.

The integration of personal values with philanthropic goals offers perhaps the most insightful model for redefining individual success. For Melinda French Gates, philanthropy is deeply personal—a reflection of her core beliefs and aspirations. This fusion of personal conviction with impactful action serves as a guide for others contemplating their legacy. By aligning her financial resources with her vision for change, Gates provides a blueprint for how individuals can achieve fulfillment through purpose-driven giving. As readers reflect on their potential legacies, they might consider how their actions today could shape future realities.

Incorporating guidelines into our reflections becomes vital in this context, particularly around the idea of legacy. It invites readers to introspect and consider their contributions beyond mere financial success. Reflecting on one's legacy encourages a deeper understanding of the impact we each choose to leave behind. Unlike transient markers of conventional wealth, a thoughtfully defined legacy represents enduring success measured by lives touched and societal advancements spurred. This guided reflection ensures that readers are inspired to evaluate and act upon aspects of their life that resonate with both personal values and societal needs.

Through her pioneering efforts, Melinda French Gates invites us all to redefine what wealth means. Her unique perspective, showcased by her focus on global health, education, gender equality, collaboration, and the alignment of personal values with philanthropic pursuits, extends a profound lesson in how true success can be achieved. As we ponder her contributions, we're reminded that wealth, when utilized as a catalyst for positive change, transcends its monetary form and becomes a testament to human potential and purpose.

Taking Action: Reflecting on Legacy and Crafting a Mission Statement

Developing a personal mission is an invaluable process that can lead to profound self-discovery and greater success. When embarking on this journey, taking the time to reflect on one's desired legacy provides a strong foundation. This reflection encourages you to look inward and consider what you truly want to leave behind. What do you want people to remember about you? What impact do you wish to make in your family, community, or even the world? By answering these questions, you begin to illuminate a path toward meaningful objectives. These long-term goals become more tangible as you envision the mark you wish to leave on the world.

Once the vision of your legacy comes into focus, crafting a mission statement becomes an essential step. A personal mission statement acts as a compass, aligning daily actions with core values and future aspirations. It encapsulates who you are, what you stand for, and where you are heading. Writing a mission statement requires introspection and honesty, demanding that you consider what matters most to you. For example, if you value innovation and creativity, your mission statement might emphasize pushing boundaries and exploring new ideas. Or, if community service is central to your values, the statement may focus on contributing positively to society. The key is to ensure that your mission statement resonates personally and reflects both your principles and your ambitions.

As life evolves, so too should your mission statement. Regularly revisiting and revising it ensures its relevance and adaptability over time.

Think of your mission as a living document—something that grows and changes alongside you. Periodic reflection allows you to assess whether your current path aligns with your stated mission. Perhaps you've experienced a significant life event that has shifted your priorities, or maybe you've learned something new about yourself that necessitates an adjustment. Consistently updating your mission statement helps prevent drift from your true objectives and keeps you grounded amid change. It also serves as a reminder of the progress you've made and the direction in which you are headed.

An often overlooked yet powerful practice is sharing your mission statement with trusted peers. Doing so enhances accountability and strengthens your commitment to your goals. Vocalizing your mission turns intangible thoughts into concrete declarations, providing opportunities for feedback and support. Sharing can be as simple as discussing your mission with a mentor, or presenting it to a group of colleagues who share similar aspirations. This openness not only bolsters your resolve but also invites others to contribute their insights and encouragement. Moreover, when others are aware of your mission, they can help hold you accountable, offering reminders and guidance when necessary.

To craft an effective mission statement, start by setting aside dedicated time for reflection. Consider journaling about your core values, strengths, and passions, identifying common themes that define your identity. Next, draft a concise statement that encapsulates these elements, being mindful to use positive and declarative language. Remember, a mission statement is meant to inspire and motivate; choose words that evoke a sense of purpose and enthusiasm.

Once your draft is complete, review it critically. Does it honestly reflect your aspirations and beliefs? Is it specific enough to guide decision-making, yet flexible enough to accommodate growth? Revising the statement is part of the process, and seeking input from trusted individuals can offer fresh perspectives and validation. As you refine your mission statement, continue asking whether it aligns with the legacy you aim to build.

Finally, embrace your mission statement as a tool for empowerment. It is not merely an abstract exercise, but a practical blueprint for achieving lasting success. By integrating this mission into everyday life, such as through decision-making or goal-setting, you create a consistent framework guiding your actions and choices. Your mission becomes a beacon during challenging times, offering clarity when faced with difficult decisions and motivation when persistence is required.

Summary and Reflections

Reflecting on the concepts shared in this chapter, it becomes evident that true success is a multifaceted journey characterized by purpose, relationships, and impact. Purpose serves as the guiding beacon, providing clarity and motivation, while aligning everyday actions with long-term goals. This alignment not only fosters a sense of fulfillment but also sharpens decision-making, ensuring each choice resonates with one's core values. Relationships form the bedrock of emotional and professional support, offering resilience and opening doors for growth. They contribute significantly to our mental well-being and happiness, enhancing both personal and communal prosperity. Lastly, impact redefines traditional measures of success by emphasizing contributions that benefit society and the environment. By prioritizing sustainable practices and positive change, individuals and organizations alike can leave lasting legacies.

The intertwined nature of purpose, relationships, and impact cultivates a holistic view of success, encouraging us to look beyond conventional definitions. Experiencing true success requires one to find meaning in their endeavors, foster meaningful connections, and make contributions that transcend individual gains. As we navigate our journeys, understanding these elements allows us to create a narrative where our dreams, values, and aspirations align harmoniously. By embracing this broader definition, we embark on a path that not only enriches our lives but also generates significant benefits for those around us. Ultimately, redefining success empowers us to strive for achievements that inspire progress and nurture human potential.

Chapter 12
Your Roadmap to Prosperity

As we reach the end of this journey, it's crucial to reflect on the vital principles we've explored and how they apply to our fast-paced, ever-changing world. These principles serve as a foundational guide — a roadmap for navigating the often tumultuous path toward personal and financial success. We've delved deeply into strategies that are both timeless and adaptable to the shifting landscapes of today's society. From entrepreneurship and career advancement to personal development and resilience, these elements interconnect, creating a robust framework for prosperity.

Today's world is characterized by volatility, uncertainty, complexity, and ambiguity. Despite these challenges, the core principles discussed in this book remain relevant and powerful. Adapting to change and embracing innovation are not just options; they have become necessities. Whether through leveraging technology or cultivating soft skills, success hinges on one's ability to pivot and thrive amid disruption. Thus, it is pertinent that every principle presented here is internalized and adapted to fit the unique contours of your personal goals and circumstances.

Yet, principles without action yield little fruit. So, let's talk about the next steps. It's time for you to take the reins of your destiny fully. Begin by setting tangible, realistic goals. Break down larger objectives into manageable tasks with clear timelines. By aligning your actions with your aspirations, you create a deliberate path toward achieving them. Remember, progress may be slow at times, and setbacks are inevitable, but perseverance beyond adversity differentiates those who succeed from those who do not.

Armed with knowledge and strategies, it is now your responsibility to implement them. Engage actively in self-improvement. Whether acquiring new technical skills, enhancing communication abilities, or expanding your professional network, each step taken contributes to building a more empowered version of yourself. Maintain an open mindset, welcoming feedback and learning from failures instead of fearing them. In a rapidly evolving world, continuous improvement stands as one of the most reliable guarantors of long-term success.

Beyond individual efforts, sharing knowledge and experiences amplifies the impact of our collective journey. I urge you to share your triumphs and challenges with others, inspiring and empowering those around you. Sharing creates ripples of motivation, encouragement, and camaraderie among individuals striving for similar goals. Whether through mentorship, public speaking, writing, or simply engaging in candid discussions, spreading insights benefits everyone by fostering environments ripe for growth.

But why stop there? Consider becoming part of a community filled with ambitious, like-minded individuals seeking personal and professional growth. Communities foster collaboration and innovation, providing platforms for exchanging ideas and forging connections. Imagine being surrounded by people who inspire, challenge, and support your vision — individuals who celebrate victories alongside you and offer guidance when faced with obstacles. Together, you can accelerate each other's journeys, drawing strength from communal wisdom.

To facilitate such connections, numerous forums, meetups, and digital platforms exist where you can quickly engage with communities tailored to your interests. Seek out groups aligned with your ambitions, participate actively, and remember that contributing to these networks is as valuable as receiving from them. The spirit of collaboration will enrich your pursuit of success and provide invaluable perspectives and resources.

As you embark on this formidable journey, armed with newly acquired knowledge and inspired by stories of those who have walked the path before you, always hold onto the belief in your potential. Your background, past experiences, or current circumstances do not determine your future trajectory — your dedication, adaptability, and willingness to learn do. Let passion drive you, and let resilience sustain you. Trust that, over time, the seeds you sow today will grow into a flourishing garden of achievements.

This book has laid out a comprehensive pathway tailored for those yearning for success. It draws from the failures, victories, lessons, and insights gathered throughout various fields and industries. Now, the onus lies with you to traverse this roadmap, discovering opportunities and realizing dreams along the way. So go forth with confidence, equipped with the tools required for this adventure. Each chapter of your life is unwritten, waiting for you to pen its story.

Remember, the quest for success is rarely linear. Instead, it's filled with twists, turns, peaks, and valleys. Embrace the unpredictability because therein lies inherent beauty. As you navigate your personal roadmap to prosperity, savor each milestone achieved, and cherish each moment of clarity discovered. For it is these experiences that ultimately craft true fulfillment and enriched lives.

You are standing at the precipice of endless possibilities. Embrace that promise and let nothing deter you from achieving greatness. This is your journey. You hold the map; you choose the destination. With courage and conviction, there is no limit to what you can accomplish. Here's to a future bright with achievements, inspired by purpose, and guided by principles that stand strong despite the tests of time.

www.ingramcontent.com/pod-product-compliance
Lightning Source LLC
Chambersburg PA
CBHW020654220526
45464CB00001B/433